ENDANGERED COLORING BOOK
OF ENDANGERED SPECIES AROUND THE WORLD

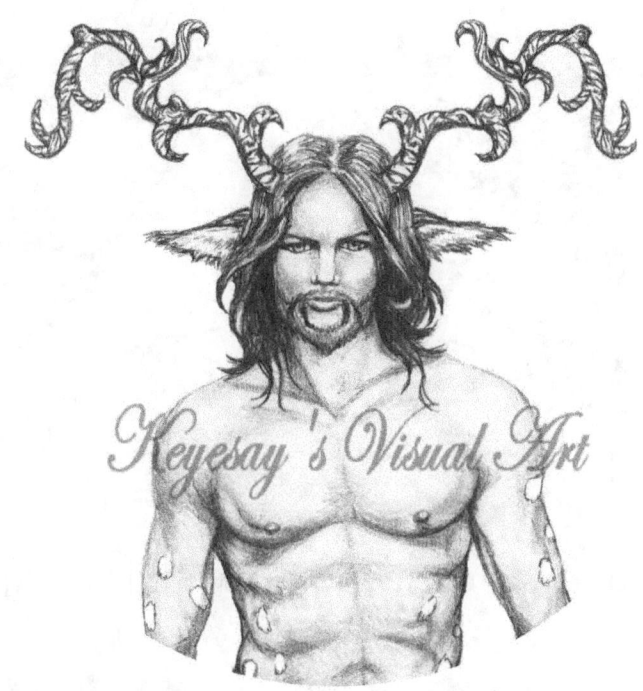

Artwork by Casey "Keyesay" Gilmore

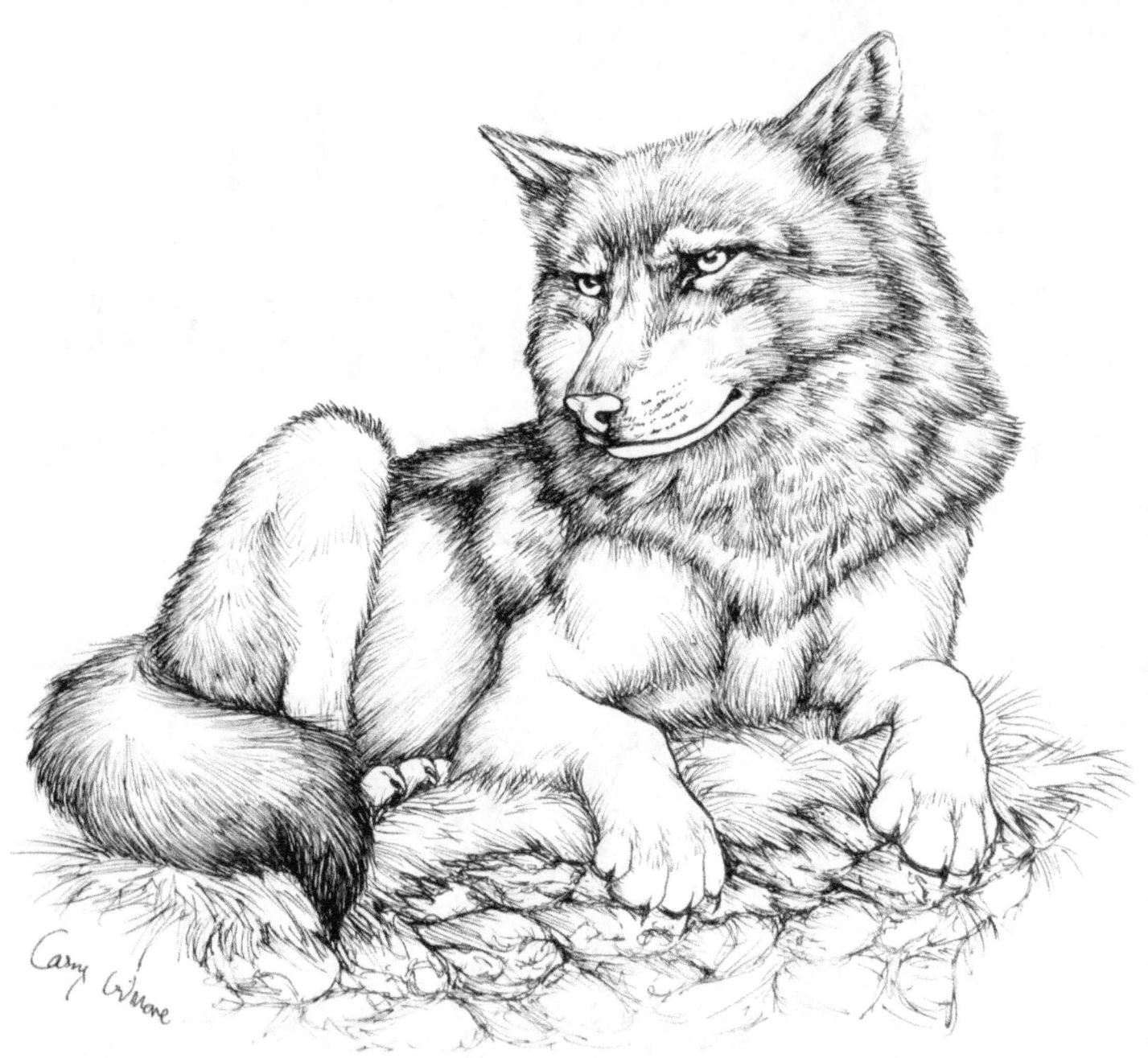

All designs are hand drawn by Casey

ENDANGERED
COLORING BOOK
Of Endangered Species Around
The World

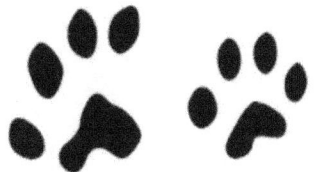
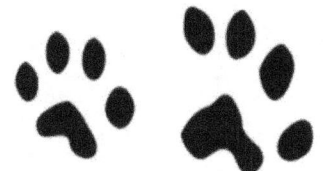

ISBN-13: 978-1530860340

ISBN-10: 1530860342

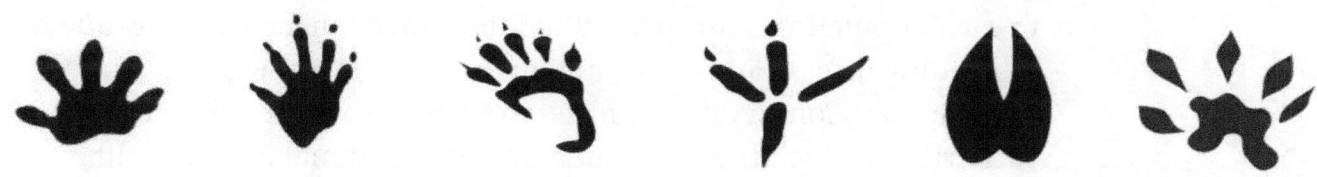

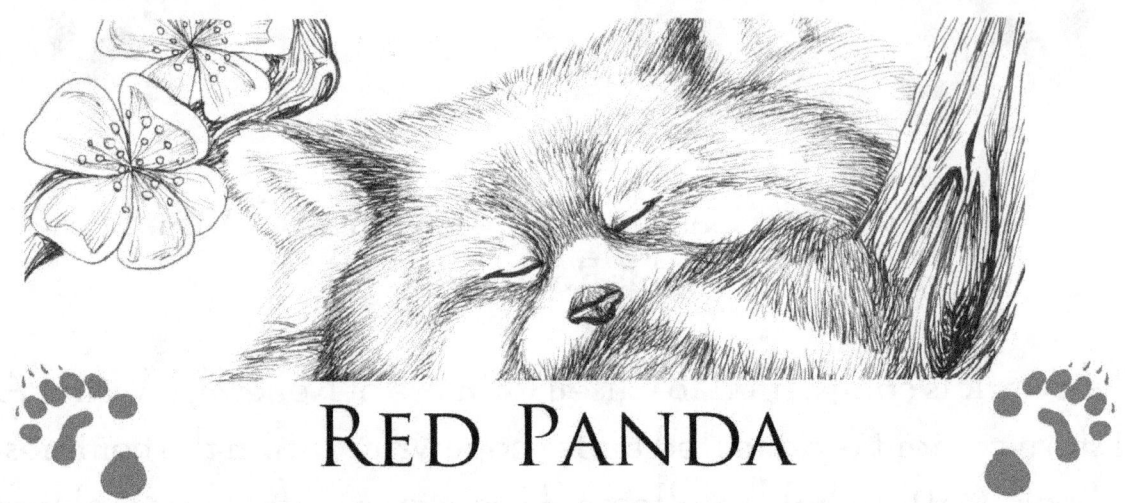

RED PANDA

SCIENTIFIC NAME: *AILURUS FULGENS*

HABITAT: Two subspecies are endemic to temperate forests of the Himalayan Mountains, and west into Nepal and eastward to China.

DIET: Mostly bamboo with supplements of bird eggs, small mammals, berries and flowers.

COLORATION: Reddish brown fur on their dorsal side, with dark brown on their ventral including their stomach, chest, and legs. Their tail has alternating rings of pale yellowish brown and the same reddish brown on their backs. Their faces have white patches on their cheeks and muzzle.

UNIQUENESS: They have long semi-retractible claws that aid them in their mostly aboreal lifestyle. They have a false thumb "digit" that helps them to grasp bamboo much like the Giant Panda (not closely related).

CONSERVATION: Its estimated that there are roughly only 10,000 mature individuals of both subspecies, and continues to decline due to habitat loss, poaching, fragmentation and inbreeding. Inbreeding due to fragmentation of their habitat caused by habitat loss is a great threat to each population's survival. When the genetic diversity is low due to inbreeding disease and environmental pressures can wipe out entire populations. Conservation efforts vary greatly between the various countries in which the Red Panda unhabits and makes an overall conservative effort hard to accomplish.

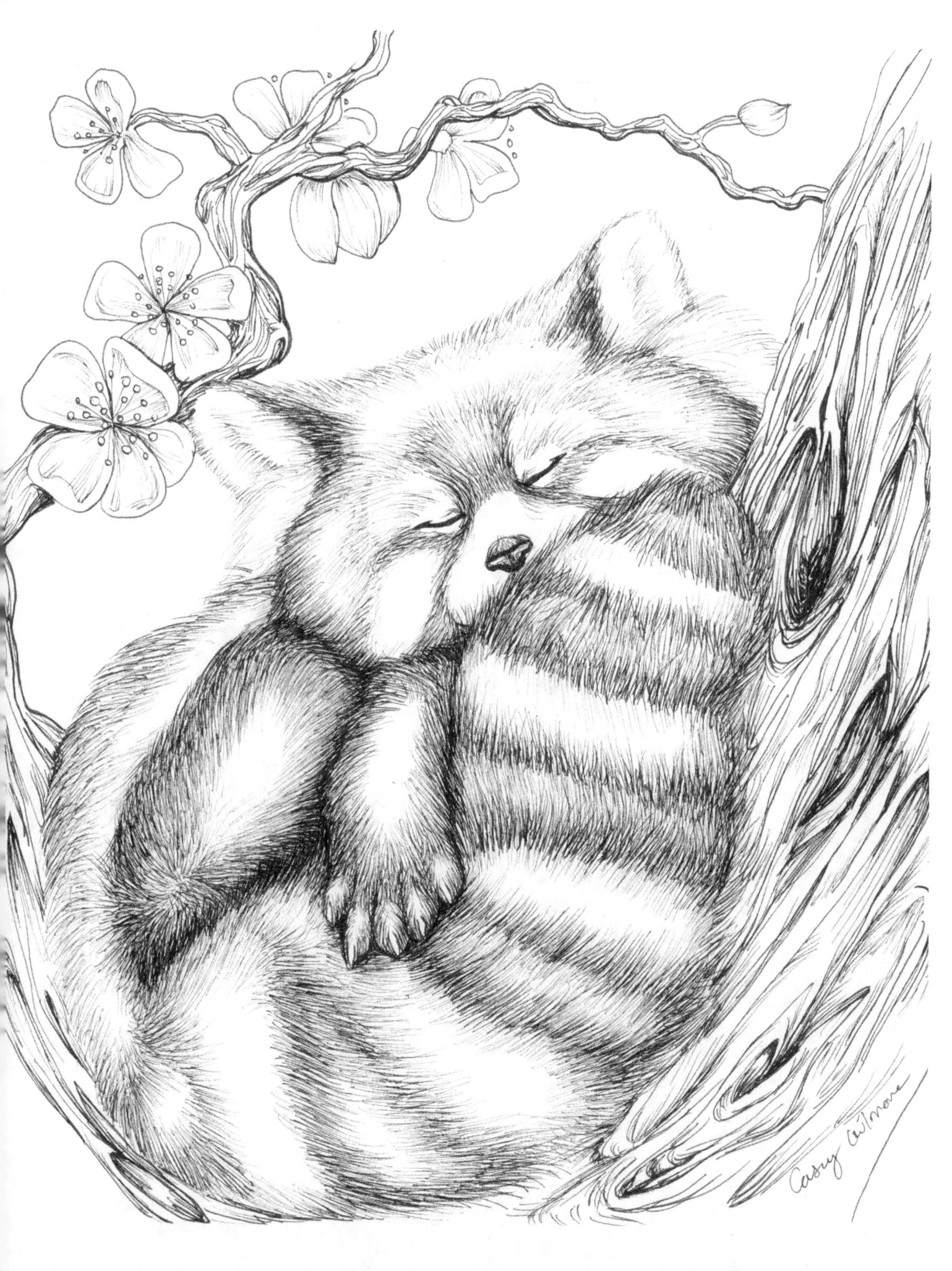

COLOR LOG

THIS IS YOUR SPACE TO TEST COLOR SCHEMES AND LOG
WHAT COLORS YOU USED FOR THE PAGES INSIDE THE
BOOK. HAVE FUN AND EXPERIMENT !!

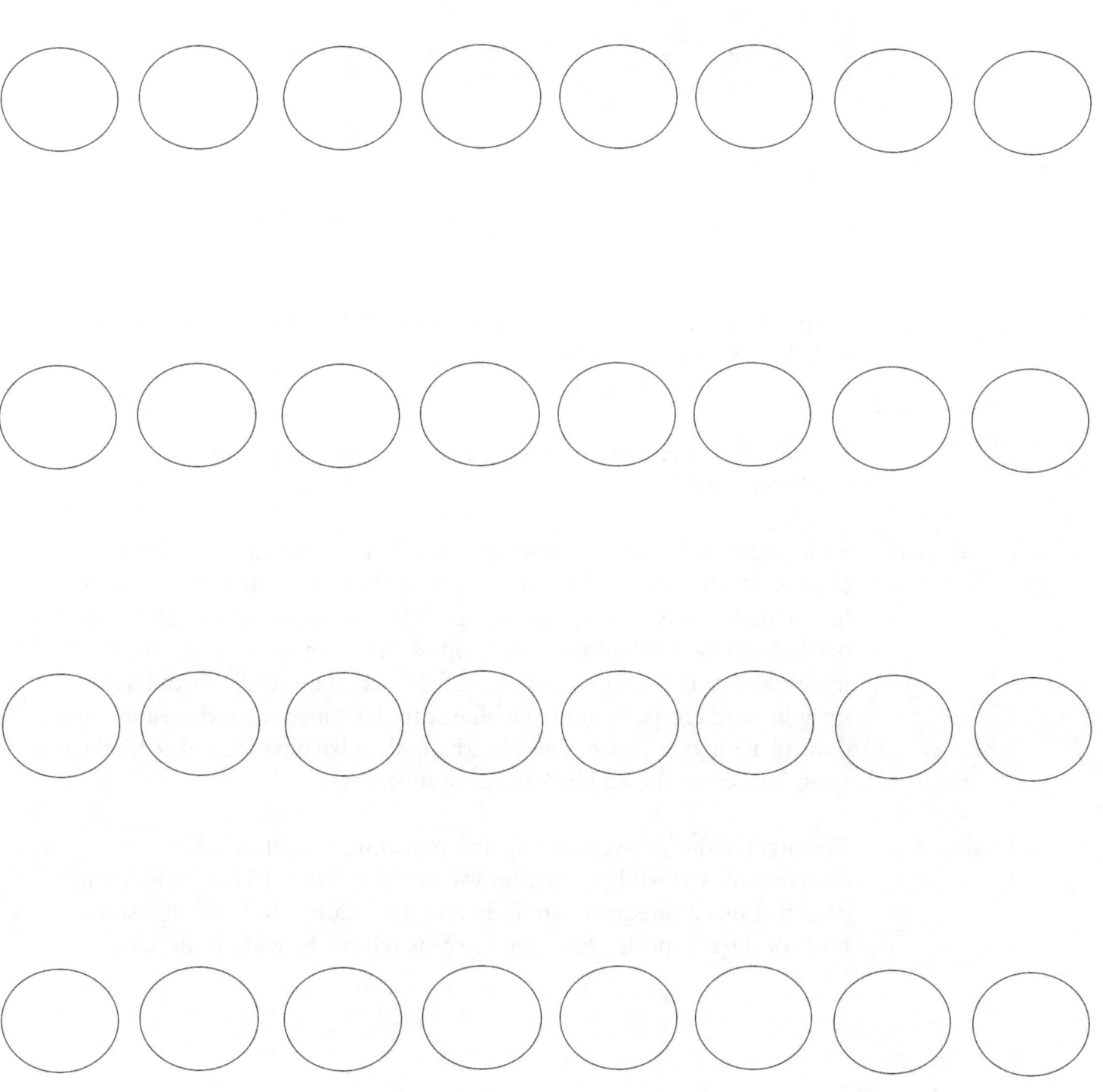

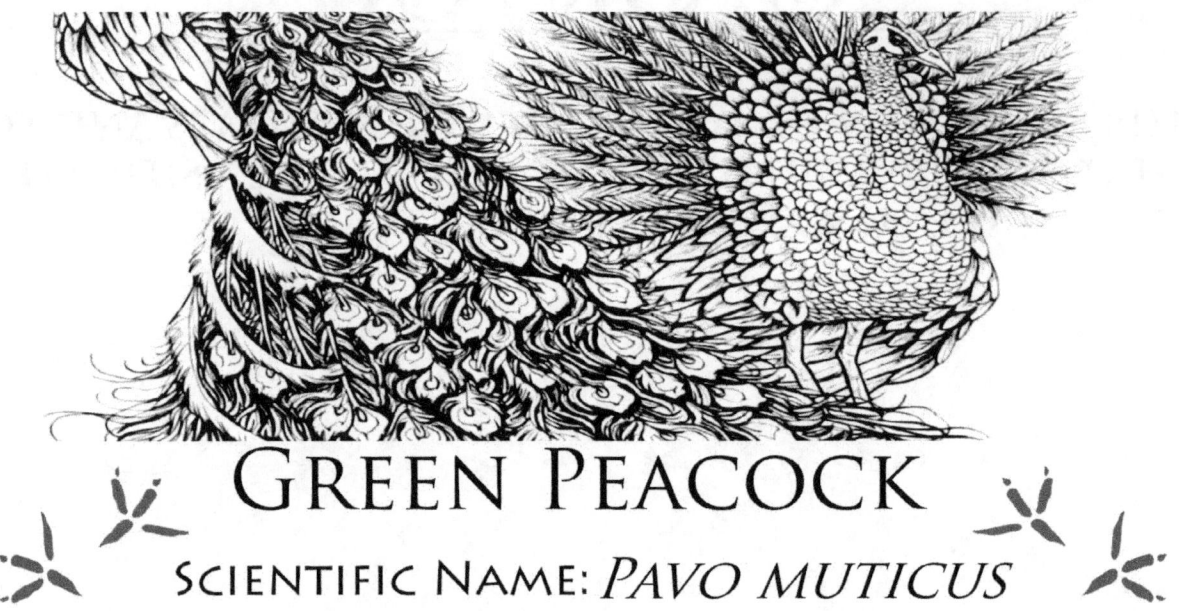

GREEN PEACOCK

SCIENTIFIC NAME: *PAVO MUTICUS*

HABITAT: Tropical, ever green, and decidious forests of Southeast Asia. Sometimes called the Javan Peafowl but this is reserved for the nominate subspecies that is endemic to Java Island.

DIET: Mainly plant parts, fruits, invertebrates, reptiles, frogs, and small mammals.

COLORATION: Male and females similar in appearance. Both pocessing enlarged upper tail coverts that are called trains. Ocelli at the tips of the train are seen on the male's while the female's extends just past her tail and lacks the ocelli. Both have brightly colored iridescent green necks with only the female with an addition of also gold feathers on her neck. Both have upright head crests. Males have blue scapulars, median and greater wing coverts, with green lesser coverts. The males also have barred secondary wing feathers or are all black in some subspecies.

CONSERVATION: Endangered due to overhunting and poaching as well as habitat destruction. The wild population was roughly 5,000-10,000 individuals back in 1995 and requires an updated population count. In 2005 some birds of the subspecies *P.m. muticus* was reintroduced to Malayasia.

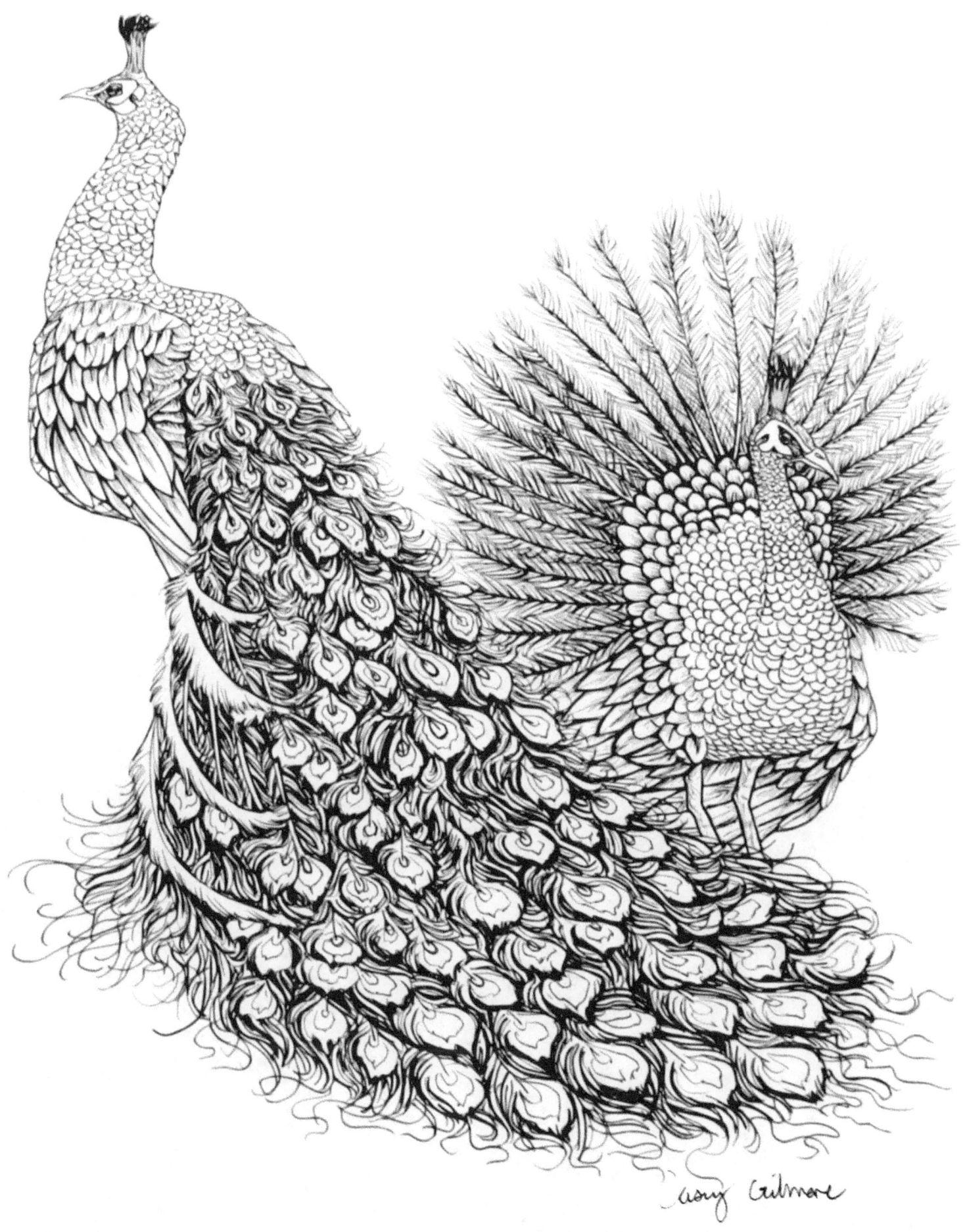

Casey Gilmore

COLOR LOG

THIS IS YOUR SPACE TO TEST COLOR SCHEMES AND LOG
WHAT COLORS YOU USED FOR THE PAGES INSIDE THE
BOOK. HAVE FUN AND EXPERIMENT !!

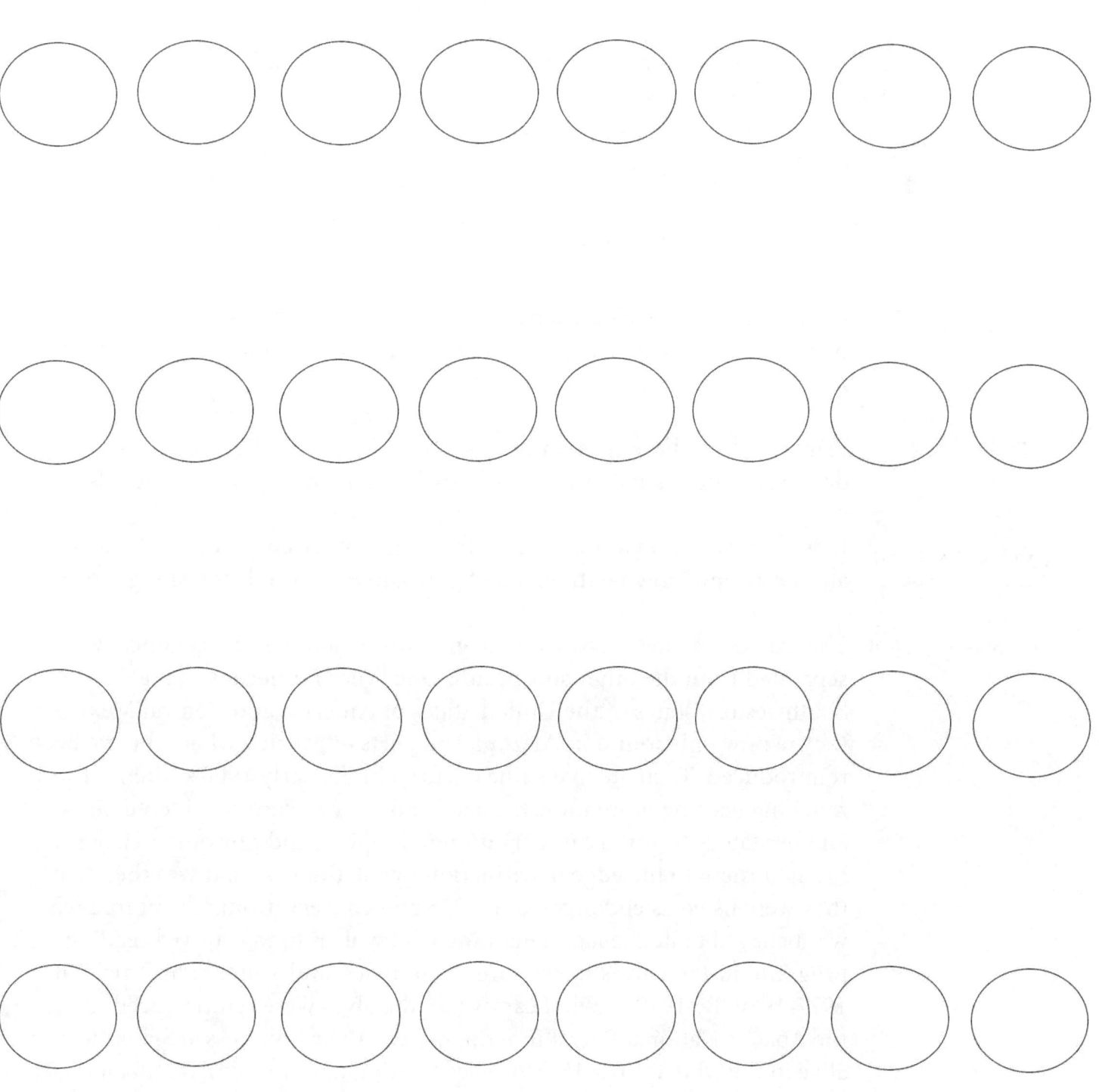

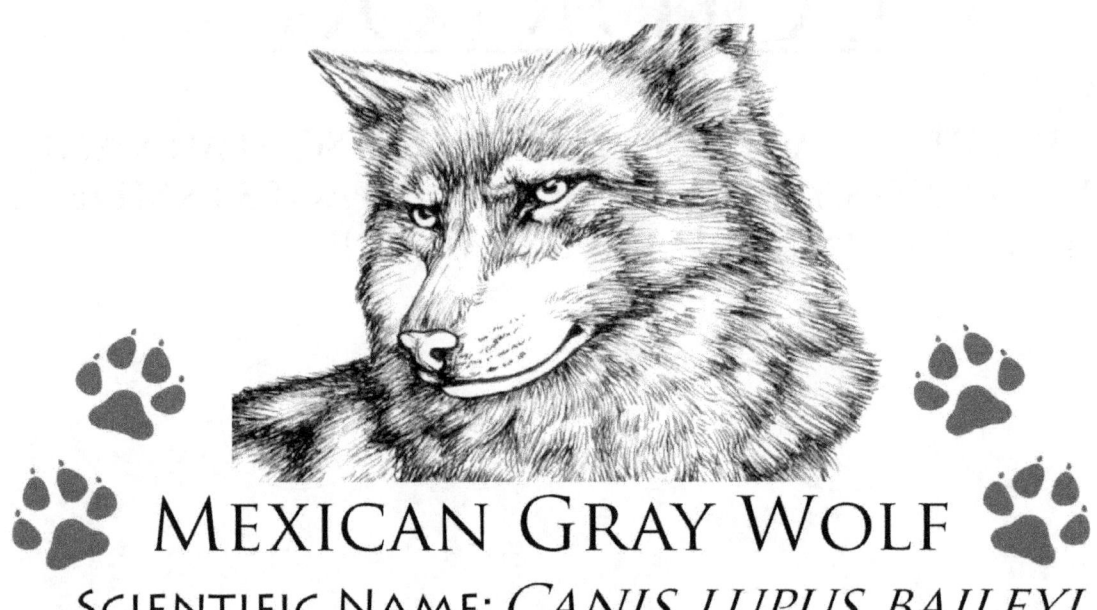

MEXICAN GRAY WOLF
SCIENTIFIC NAME: *CANIS LUPUS BAILEYI*

HABITAT: Occuring in Arizona's Apache National Forest and parts of Northwestern Mexico. Preferring grasslands, scrub lands and mountain forests.

DIET: Primarily large hooved mammals such as elf, white tailed deer, and mule deer. Sometimes smaller mammals such as hare and ground squirrels.

COLORATION: Less color variation among individuals than other gray wolves. Typically all over tawny brown with grizzled gray and patchs of black along the back.

CONSERVATION: They're the smallest subspecies of gray wolf and the most genetically separated from the other subspecies. Once very numerous in the Southwestern states of the United States of America and Central Mexico, they're now only found in Arizona and parts of Mexico where they've been reintroduced. Their steep decline occured in the early 1900's when cattle ranching became more industrialized and wolves were considered pests and predatory towards cattle. Hunting, trapping, and poisoning virtually brought them to the edge of extinction by the the 1970's. It was then that they were listed as endangered in 1976 and conservationists captured what was believed to be the last remaining wild wolves for a captive breeding program. Just 5 wolves were captured, 4 males, and 1 pregnant female in 1977-1980. By 1999 the first captive bred wolves were reintroduced to the Apache National Forest in Arizona, and their numbers are close to 100 alive in the wild as of 2015. However hunting and trapping is still an issue, and even with high fines for anyone caught poaching it still occurs regularly.

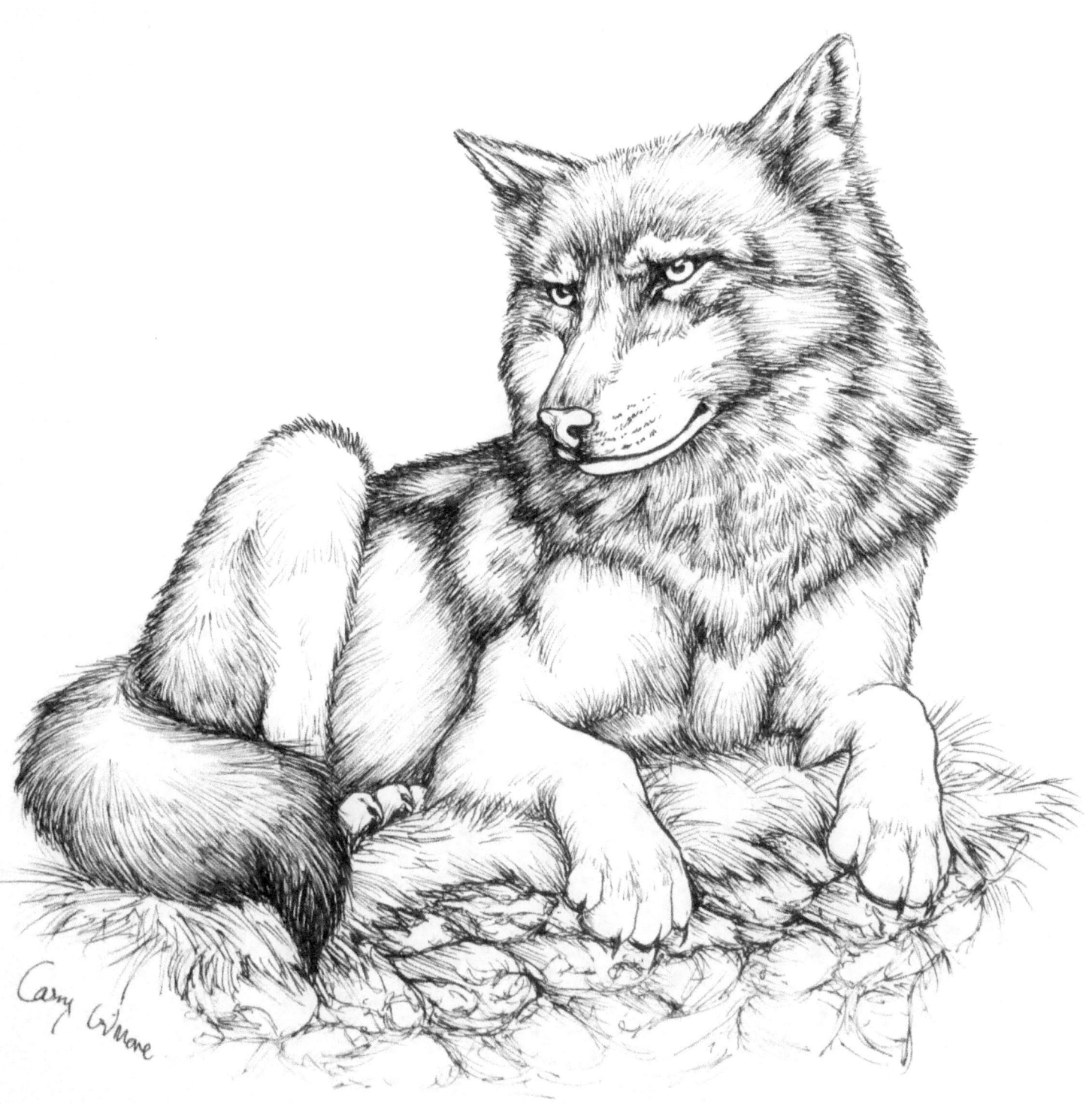

COLOR LOG

THIS IS YOUR SPACE TO TEST COLOR SCHEMES AND LOG
WHAT COLORS YOU USED FOR THE PAGES INSIDE THE
BOOK. HAVE FUN AND EXPERIMENT !!

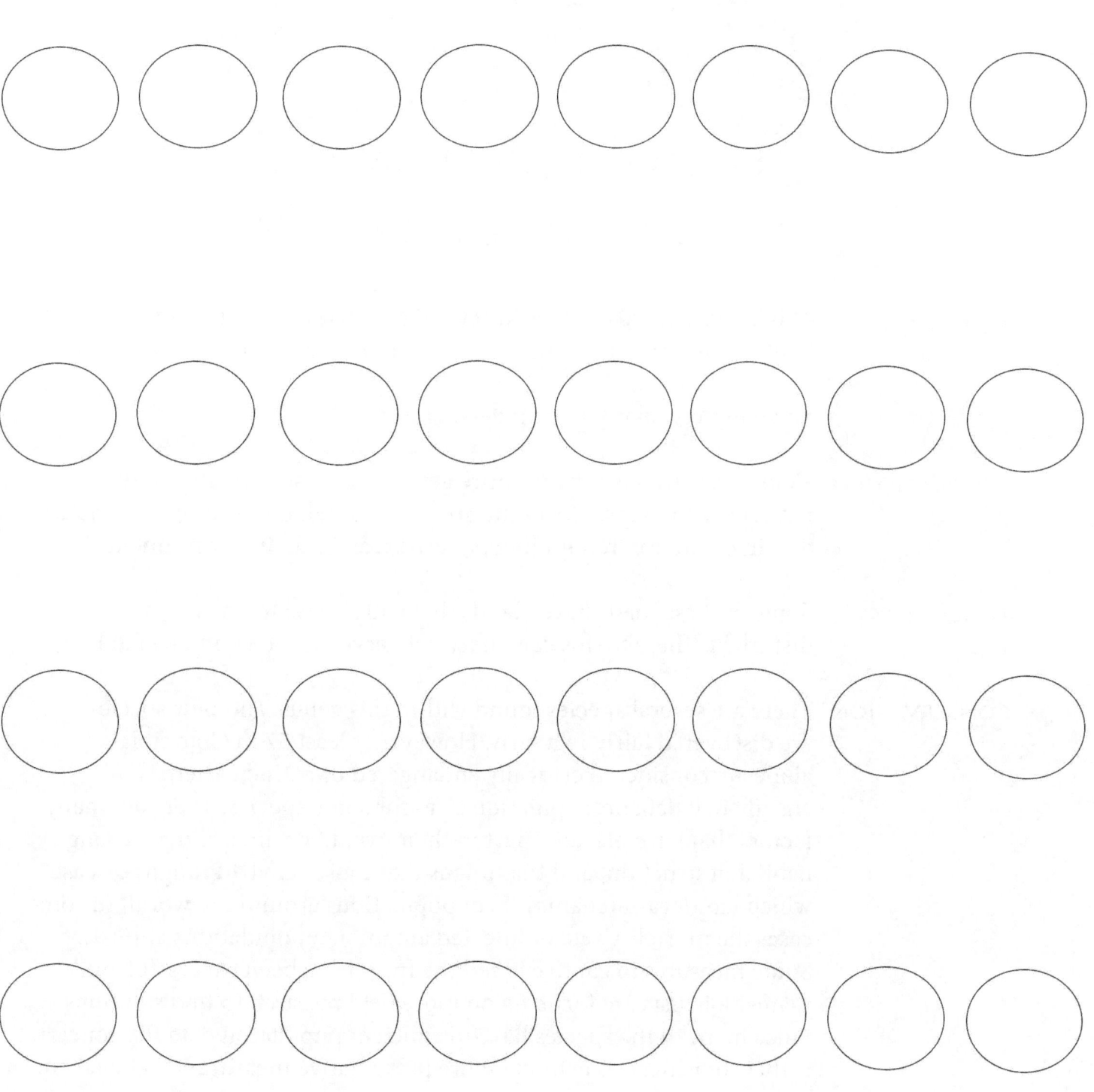

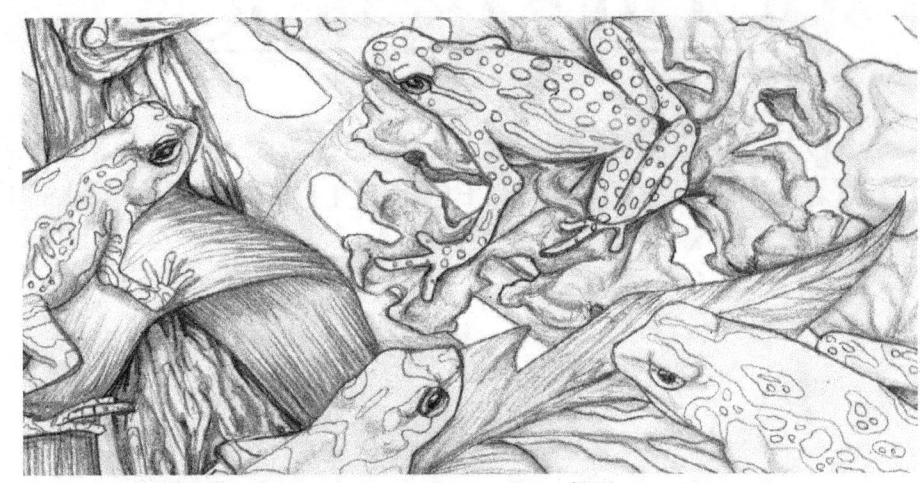

Harlequin Toads

Scientific Name: *Atelopus*

HABITAT: This genus of toads occurs in several countries of Central and South America in mid-high elevation moist habitats along streams.

DIET: Small insects, snails, and spiders.

COLORATION: Colors vary widely for the entire genus but most have distinctive patterns with loops, swirls and streaks. Though often colorful some are dull in coloration resembling patterns seen in their environment.

UNIQUENESS: Some of these toads have glands that will release toxins when disturbed. These toxins can affect the nervous system and be fatal.

CONSERVATION: There are several species found within this genus, and new species are discovered fairly regularly. However at least 37 in Columbia alone are considered critically endangered or extinct. There is ensufficient data on population sizes for some species. There are many factors that have played a part in their overall decline; climate change, habitat destruction, and the fungus that causes chytrid fungus disease which has devastatedamphibian populations around the world. In some cases the mortality rate of infected amphibian populations is 100%. Some measures to captive breed the frogs have been successful, but many biologists are focusing on more field research to find solutions. Since many of the species have insufficient population data the concern is that some may go extinct before preventative measures can be taken.

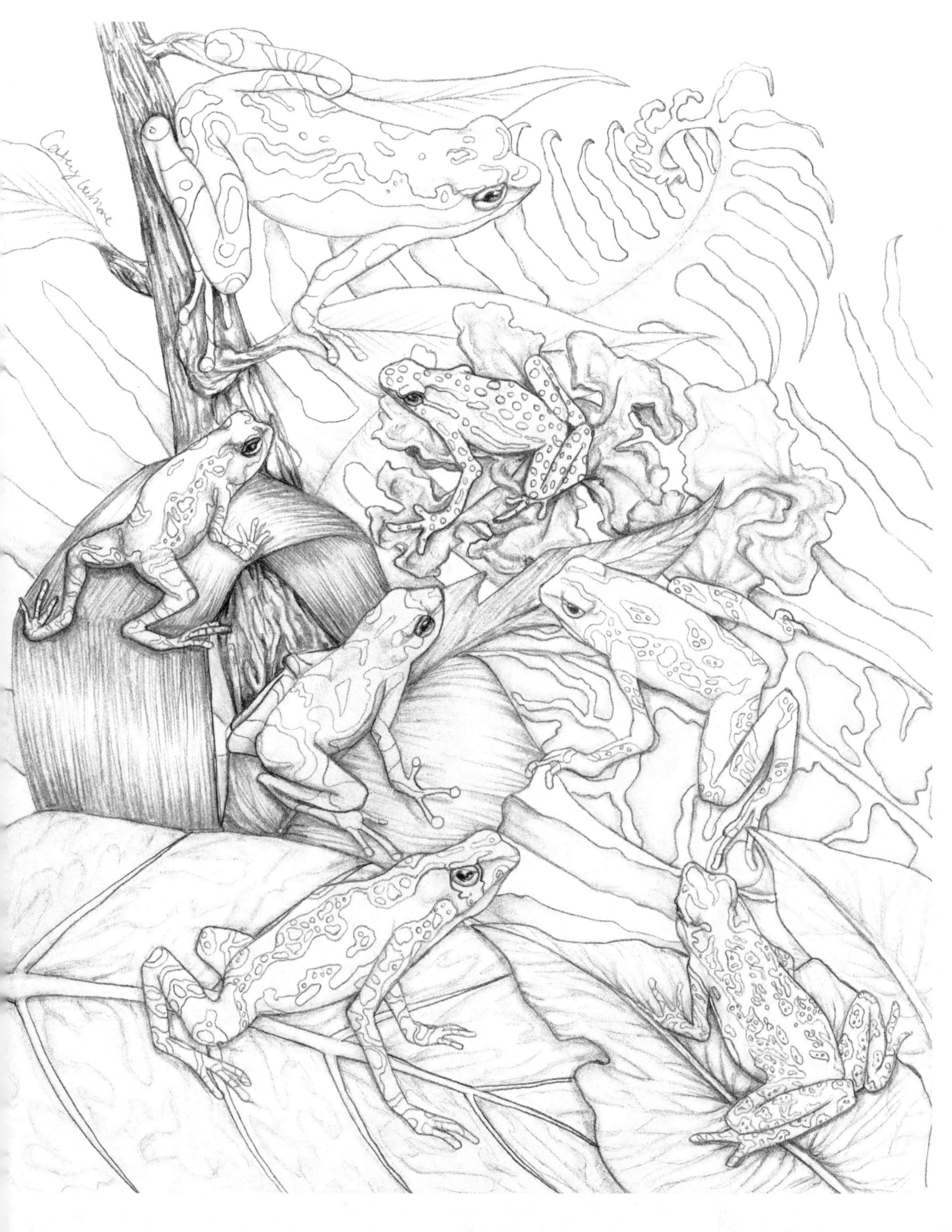

COLOR LOG

THIS IS YOUR SPACE TO TEST COLOR SCHEMES AND LOG WHAT COLORS YOU USED FOR THE PAGES INSIDE THE BOOK. HAVE FUN AND EXPERIMENT !!

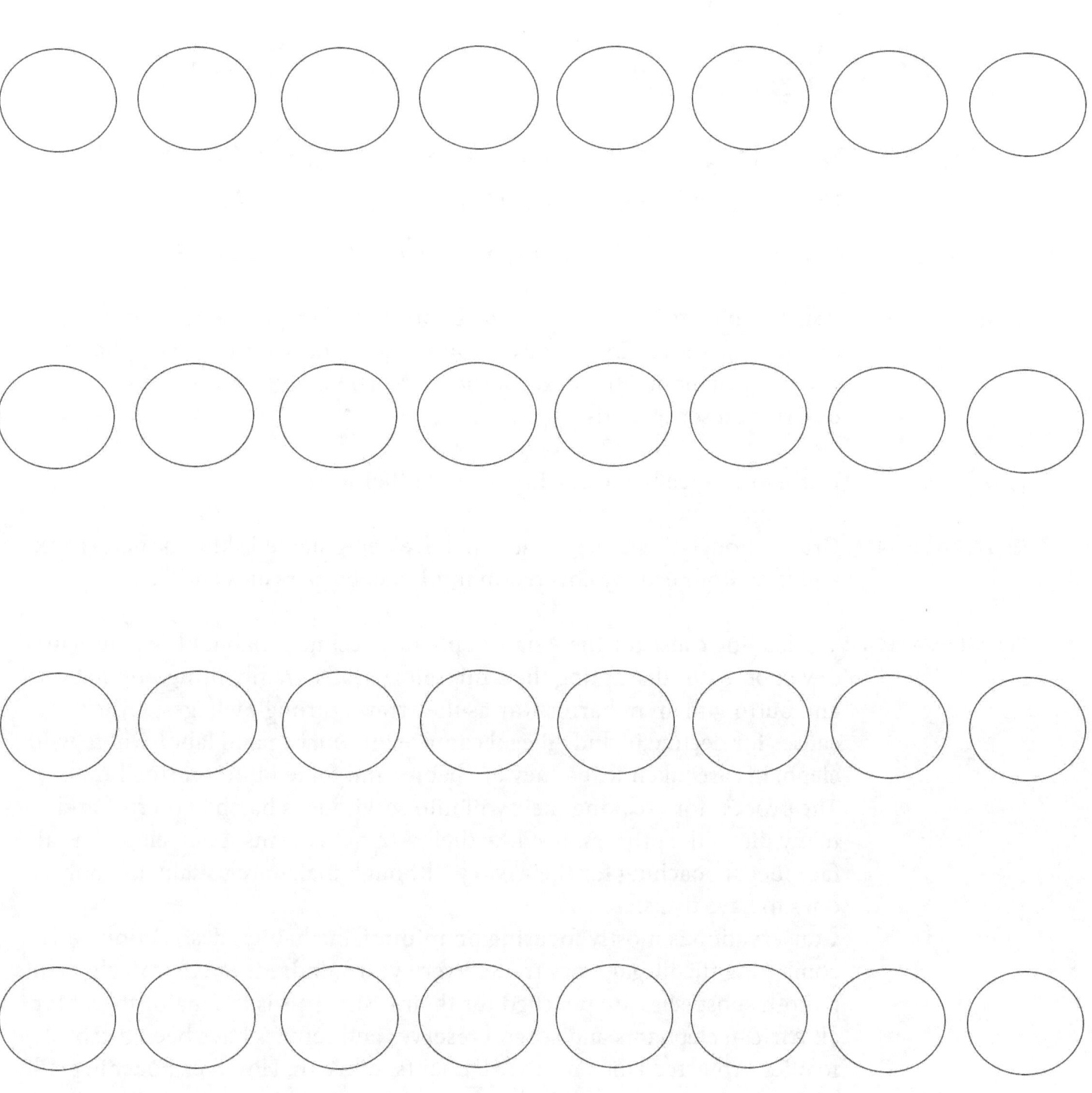

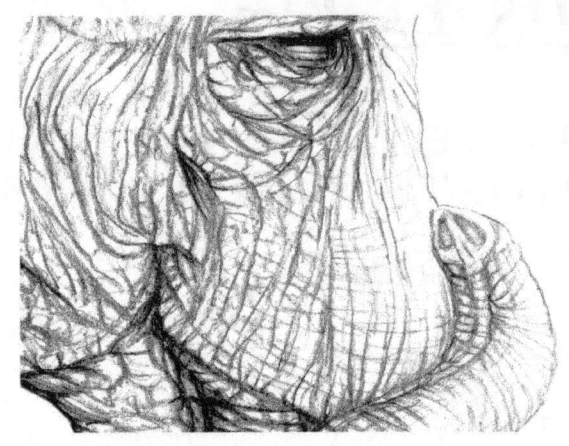
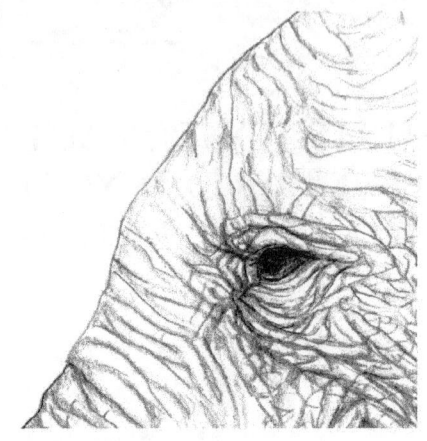

ASIAN AND AFRICAN ELEPHANTS
SCIENTIFIC NAME: *ELEPHAS MAXIMUS,*
LOXODONTA AFRICANA AND L.CYCLOTIS

HABITAT: Asian elephants inhabitat dry scrub forests and tropical evergreen forests of Sumatra, India, China and surrounding countries. African elephants occur throughout Africa except the far North; among dense forests, deserts and scrub lands.

DIET: Herbivorous feeding trees, brush, and other foliage.

COLORATION: Gray although Asian elephants can have depigmented skin on their trunks and face. Both usually covered in mud to deter parasites and flies.

CONSERVATION: The leading cause for the Asian elephant's decline is habitat loss. Human development is disrupting their migratory trails, fragmenting populations, and putting them in harms way as they travel through villages. Other causes for decline include illegal capture for tourism and labor where wild elephants are taken when they are babies and forced into serving humans. The process for breaking their will into servitude is harsh and cruel and many die in the process. Just like their African cousins Asian elephants also face illegal poaching for their ivory, although males are usually the only ones to have tusks.

Conservation is mostly focusing on minimizing habitat destruction and combating the illegal ivory trade. Every year hundreds of African elephants of both subspecies are poached for their tusks. This is the major threat for all African elephants and several reserves and refuges have been established to offer protected lands for the elephants to live in. However poaching still occurs in even protected lands.

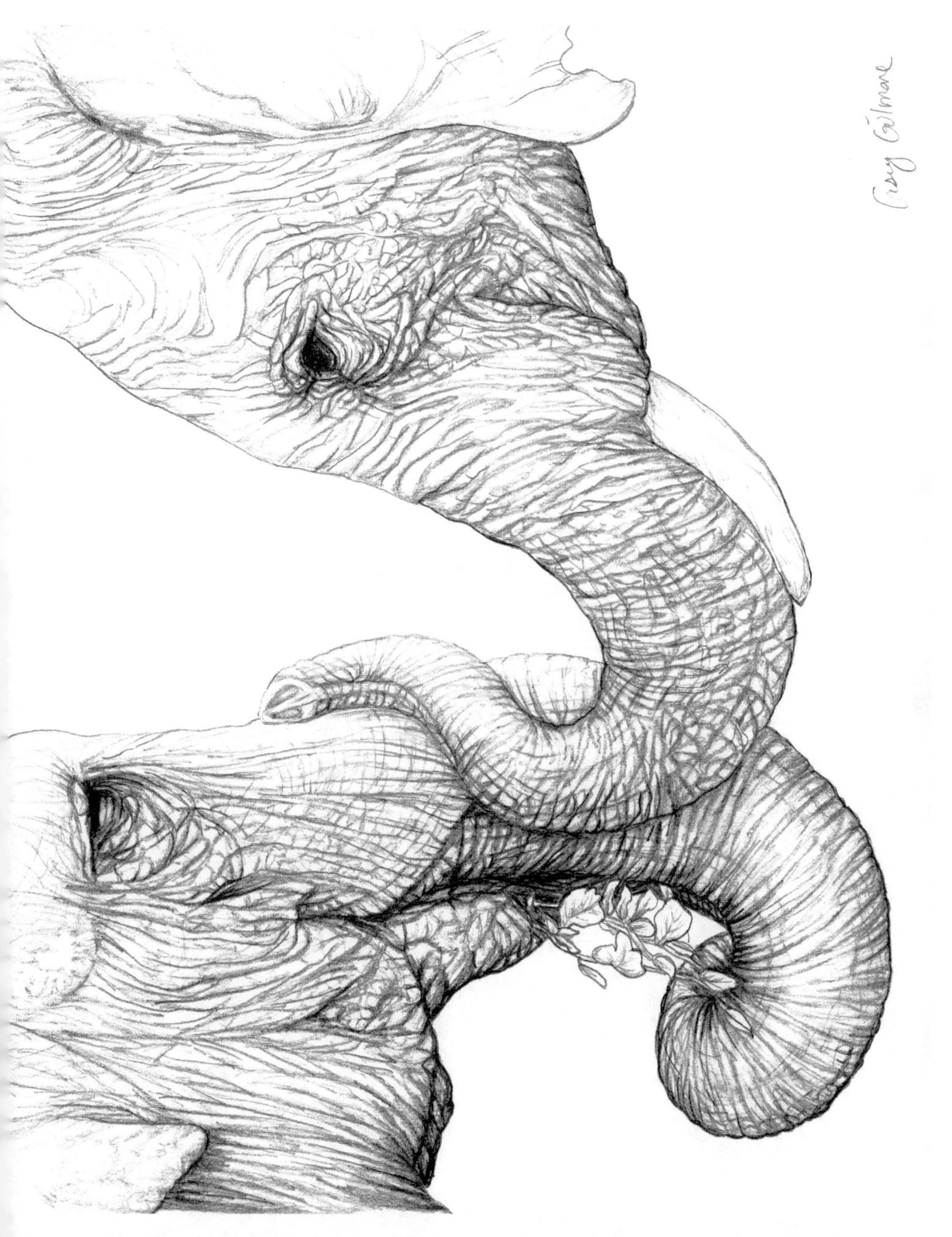

COLOR LOG

THIS IS YOUR SPACE TO TEST COLOR SCHEMES AND LOG WHAT COLORS YOU USED FOR THE PAGES INSIDE THE BOOK. HAVE FUN AND EXPERIMENT !!

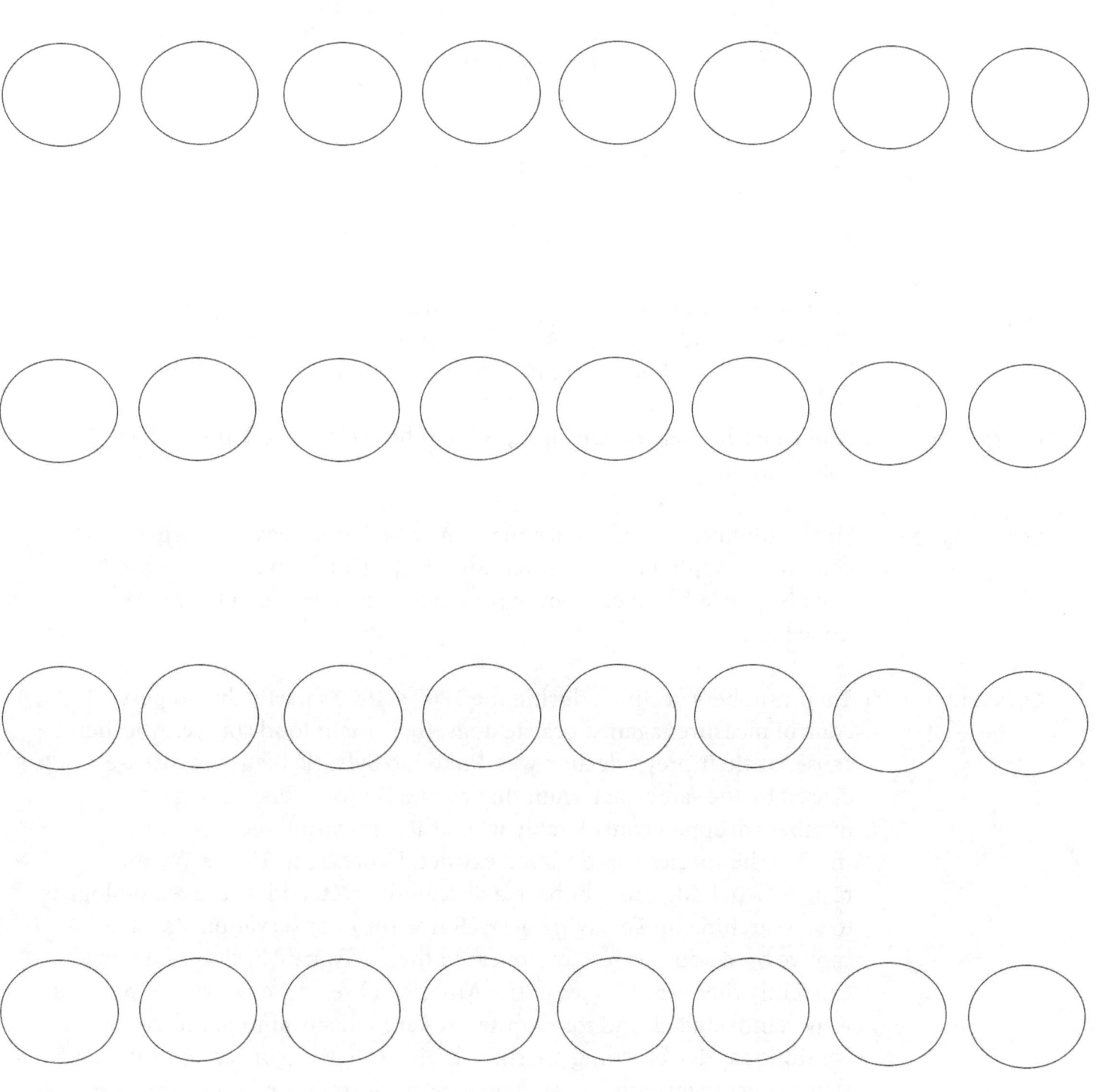

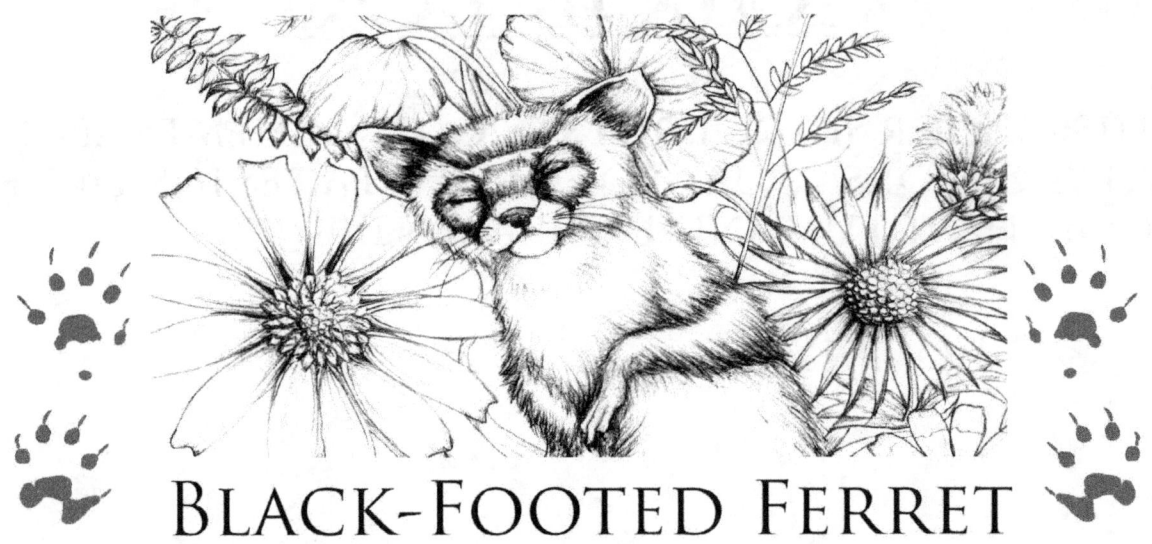

Black-Footed Ferret

Scientific Name: *Mustela nigripes*

Habitat: Short grass and mix grass prairies, shrub and sagebush steppes, some desert grasslands of North America; with reintroduced populations in Wyoming, Utah, South Dakota, Montana, Colorado, and Arizona.

Diet: Almost excluvisely prairie dogs; some other smaller rodents such as voles and mice.

Coloration: Short blunt heads with a dark mask over the eyes. Legs darker in coloration ranging from a cinnamon brown to a deep chocolate brown. Back is grizzled with cinnamon brown and cream; with a long dark tipped tail.

Conservation: Their numbers declined during the 1800's-1900's partly due to pest control measures against prairie dogs; their main food source. Another cause for their prey's decline was linked to Sylvatic Plague, a disease caused by the same bacterium that causes Bubonic Plague. Ferret numbers dropped considerably when their prey suffered a decline. In 1979 the species was declared extinct. However in 1981 a Wyoming resident's pet dog brought back a deceased ferret, and it spurred biologists to go searching for surviving nests. Since 1987 conservationists have captive bred adult ferrets and released their offspring back into the wild. Currently there are 18 sites in the American West where ferret populations were reintroduced, and four of the sites are self sustaining. Efforts to continue captive breeding are still a major role that conservationists and state governments are focusing on as some ferret populations aren't self sustaining yet. There are roughly a 1000 adult ferrets in the wild.

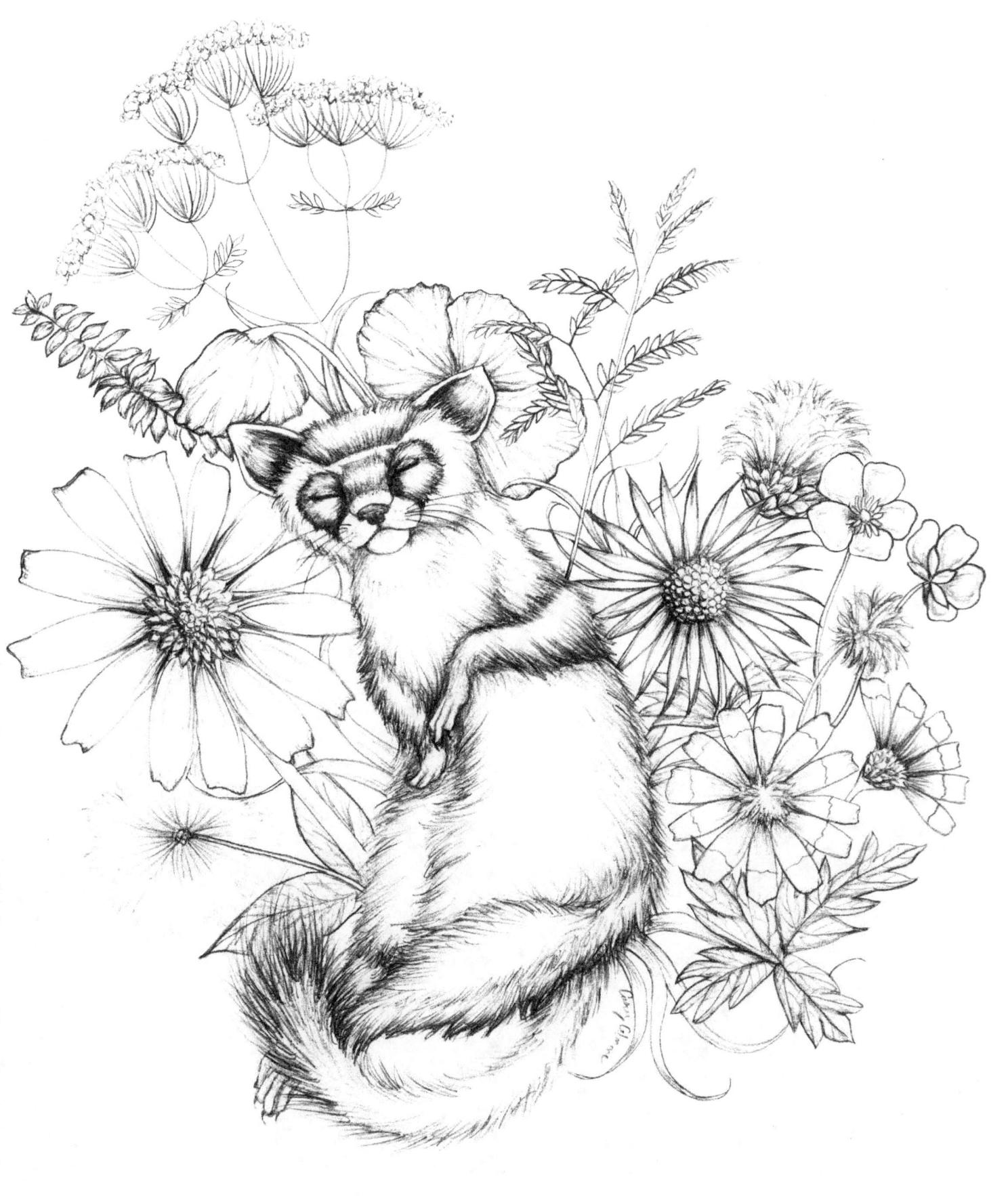

COLOR LOG

THIS IS YOUR SPACE TO TEST COLOR SCHEMES AND LOG
WHAT COLORS YOU USED FOR THE PAGES INSIDE THE
BOOK. HAVE FUN AND EXPERIMENT !!

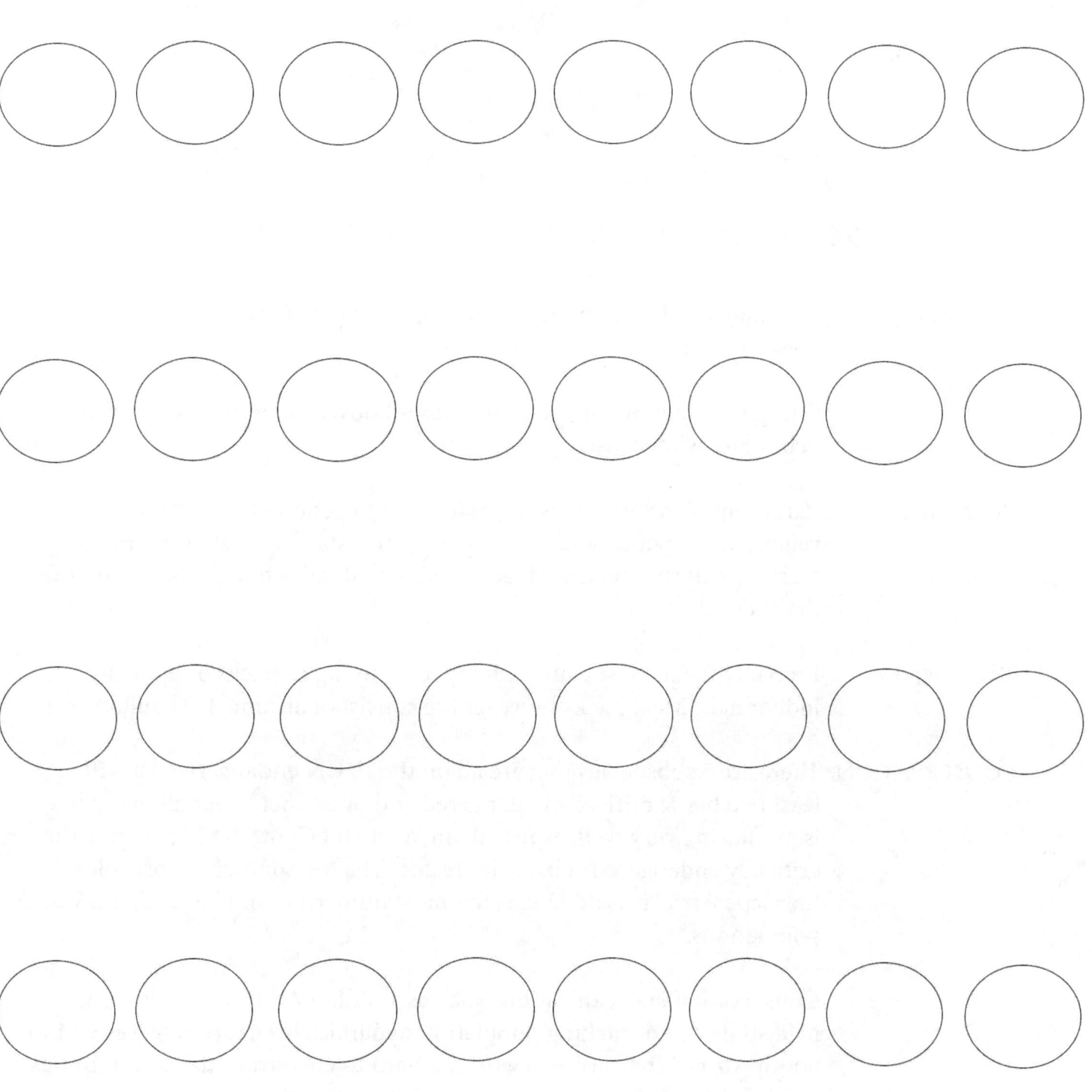

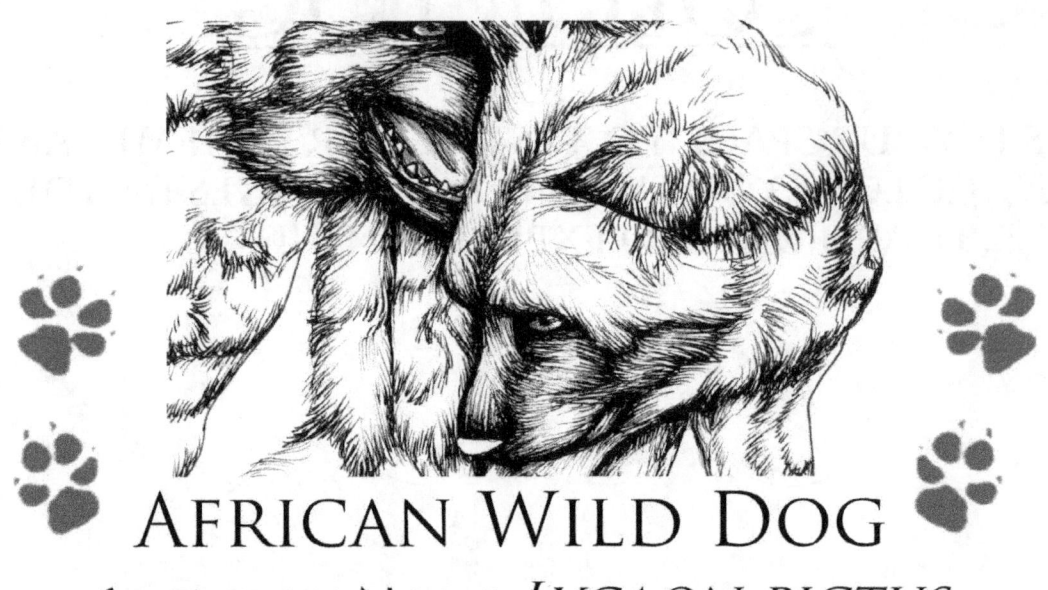

African Wild Dog
Scientific Name: *Lycaon Pictus*

Habitat: Arid lands and savannahs of Central, Southern, Eastern and Western Africa.

Diet: Gazelle, springbok, impala, sometimes hooved mammals as large as zebra and wildebeast.

Coloration: Variations in color occurs regionally but in general there is a mix of yellow, black, white, and brown patches and splotches all over. Facial markings always having a black muzzle that fades to light brown on the the cheeks.

Uniqueness: Probably the most social canine species, living in packs of up to 40 individuals. Most packs however are consist of around 4-9 adults.

Conservation: There are 5 subspecies that are all on the IUCN endangered list with at least two being critically endangered and or extinct. Over all the species is not fairing very well, especially in West and Central Africa where the critically endangered subspecies reside. The the Southern subspecies the Cape African Wild Dog is the most numerous and have several viable populations.

Conservationist organizations such as Wildlife ACT are conducting field studies and tracking population dynamics in nature reserves within South Africa. They are also working hard to encourage the communities around the nature reserves to value and protect the lands and dogs.

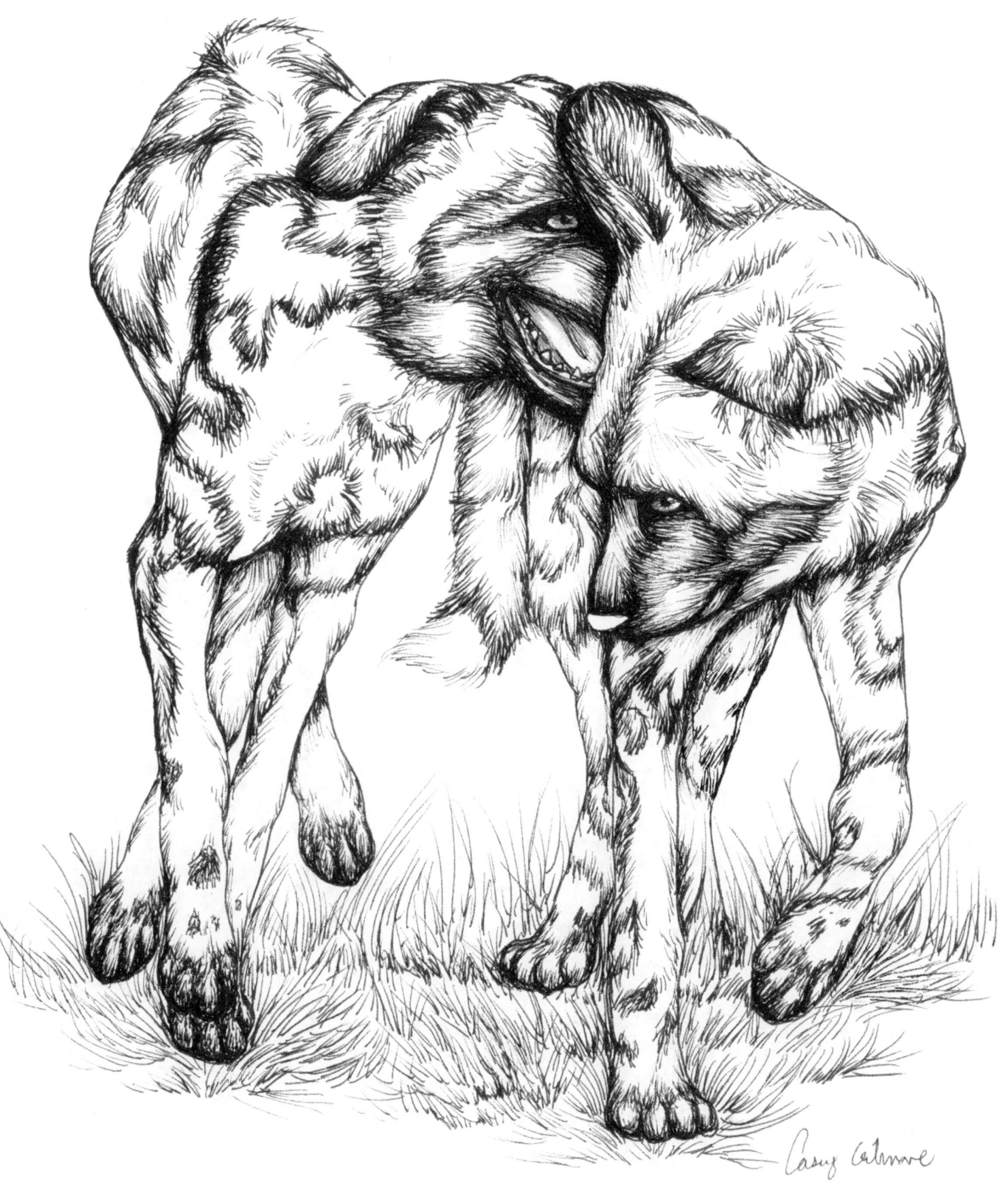

COLOR LOG

THIS IS YOUR SPACE TO TEST COLOR SCHEMES AND LOG
WHAT COLORS YOU USED FOR THE PAGES INSIDE THE
BOOK. HAVE FUN AND EXPERIMENT !!

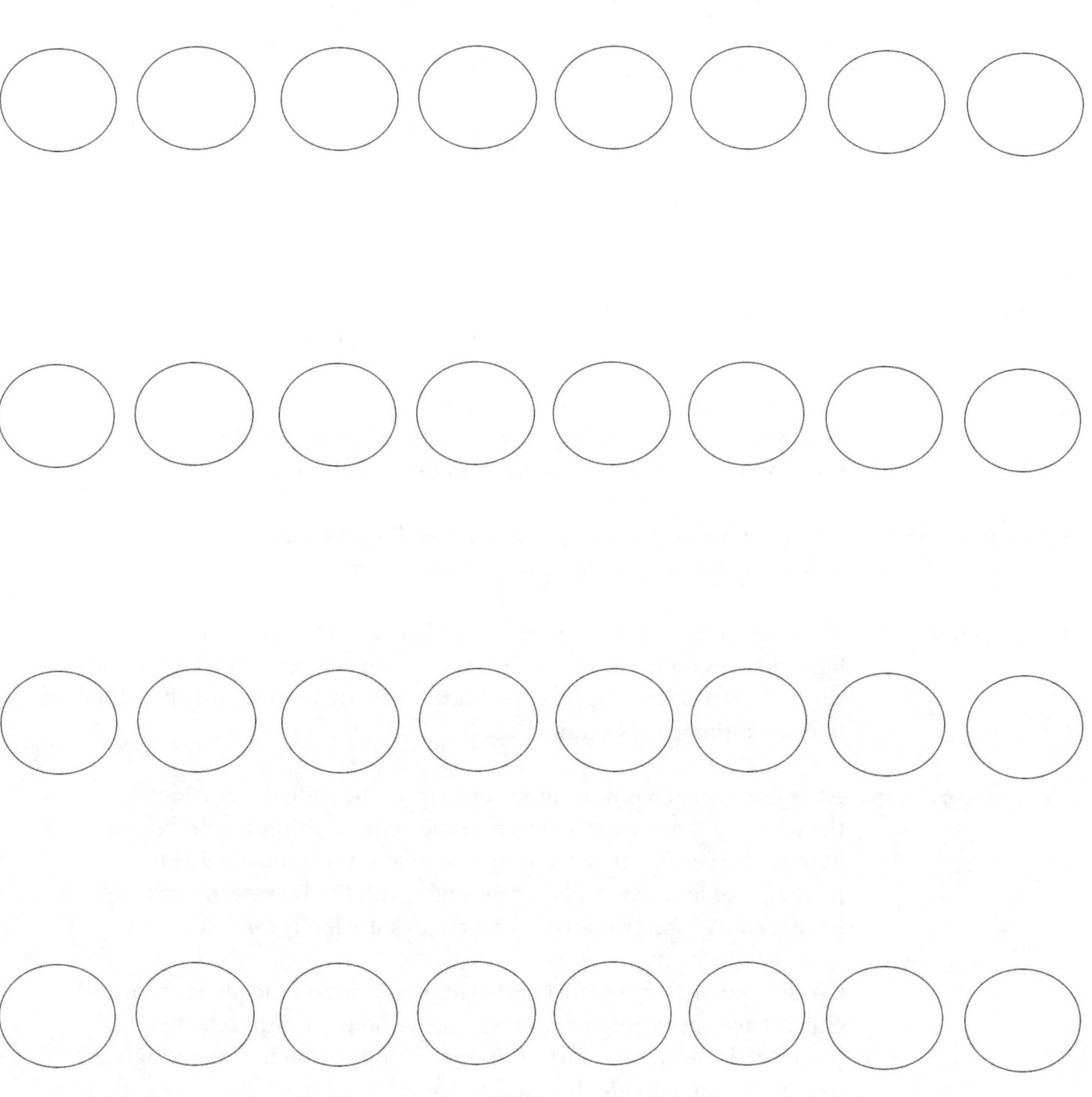

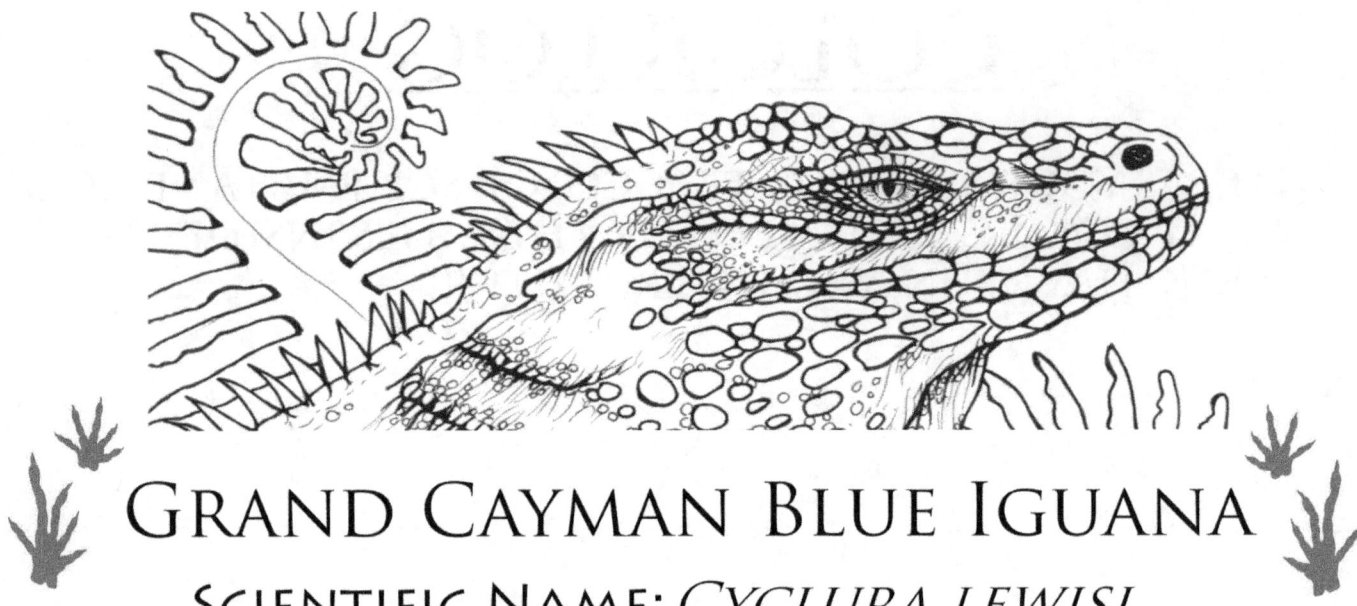

Grand Cayman Blue Iguana
Scientific Name: *Cyclura lewisi*

HABITAT: Sunlit rocky open areas, sandy beaches, and dry forests of the eastern interior of Grand Cayman.

DIET: Herbivore; flowers, succulents, and other plant material. They play an important role in seed dispersal and seeds that pass through their digestive tracts germinate faster than those that do not.

COLORATION: Dull brown and gray except during breeding season males become a more pronounced blue in coloration.

UNIQUENESS: They have a "third" eye (parietal eye) that detects movement and light changes on the top of their head. Life expendancy is long, although varies, however the longest lived lizard in captivity was Godzilla who lived to be an estimated 69 years of age.

CONSERVATION: After European colonization fewer than 15 individuals remained in the wild and it was expected to become extinct within the first decade of the 21st century. This decline in population was mostly due to predation of feral cats and dogs brought with the Europeans and from habitat conversion from fruit farms to pasture lands for cattle.

Considered one of the most endangered species on the planet conservation efforts have been centered around captive breeding and release into protected lands. Late in 2012 the species population had risen high enough, to around 700 individuals, that they were moved from critically endangered to endangered. This is all due to the hard work of conservationists and the Grand Cayman Government.

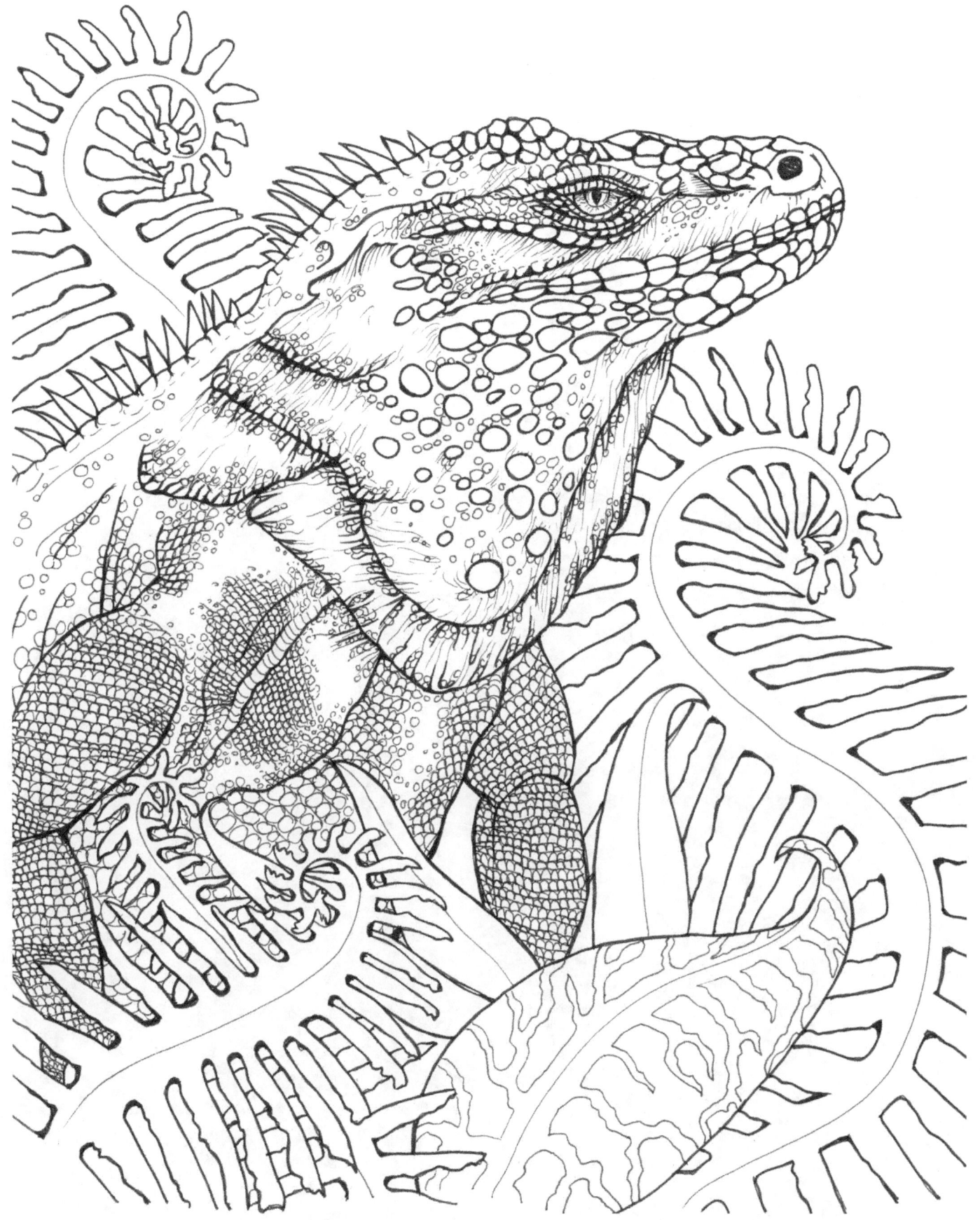

COLOR LOG

THIS IS YOUR SPACE TO TEST COLOR SCHEMES AND LOG
WHAT COLORS YOU USED FOR THE PAGES INSIDE THE
BOOK. HAVE FUN AND EXPERIMENT !!

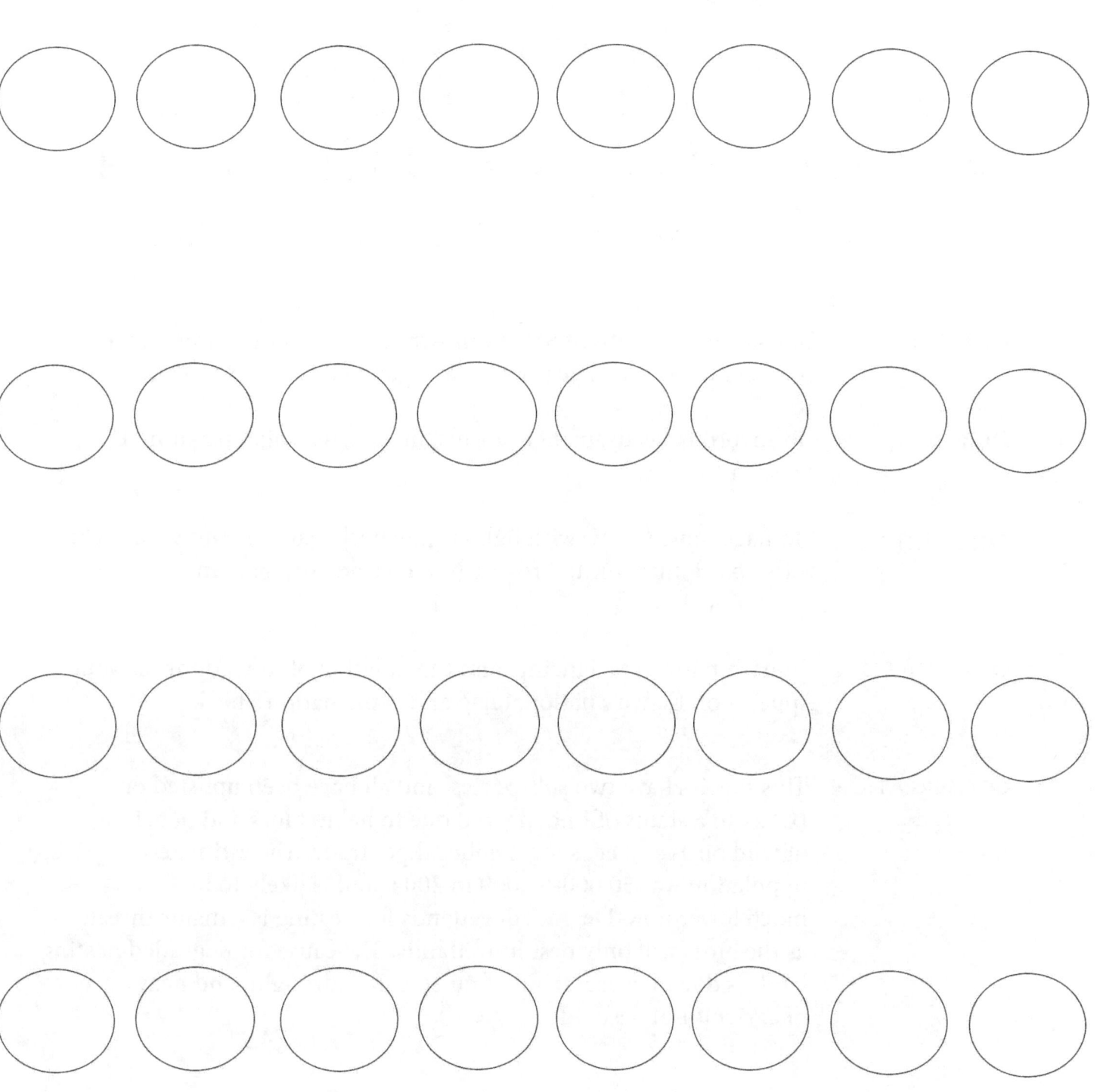

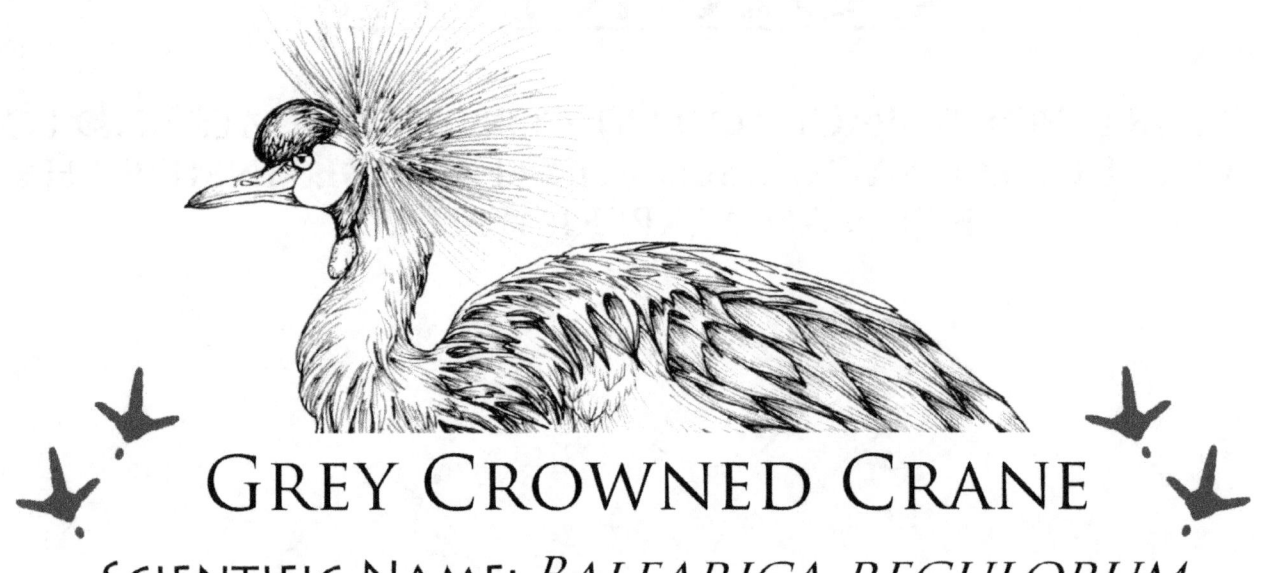

Grey Crowned Crane

Scientific Name: *Balearica regulorum*

HABITAT: Dry savannah South of Sahara in Africa. Can occur in wet marshes, cultivated grasslands near rivers of Uganda down to South Africa.

DIET: Omnivorous; seeds, plants, worms, insects, fish, aquatic animal eggs, and snakes.

COLORATION: Plumage mostly gray, with lighter gray neck feathers, and wings white with tips of maroon to brownish red. Head crest golden with red throat pouch.

UNIQUENESS: Courtship involves dancing, and the inflation of the red throat pouch. Appears on Kenya's national flag and is the nation's bird.

CONSERVATION: This species have two subspecies, and all have been uplisted on IUCN to a status of Endangered due to habitat loss and poaching of wild birds and eggs for the illegal pet trade. The estimated population was 50,000-65,000 in 2004, and is likely to be much lower now. Degraded wetlands for nesting is a major threat, as the birds will only nest in wetlands. The cause for degraded nesting lands is due to overgrazing of ranch cattle, drought, and heavy use of agricultural pesticide usage.

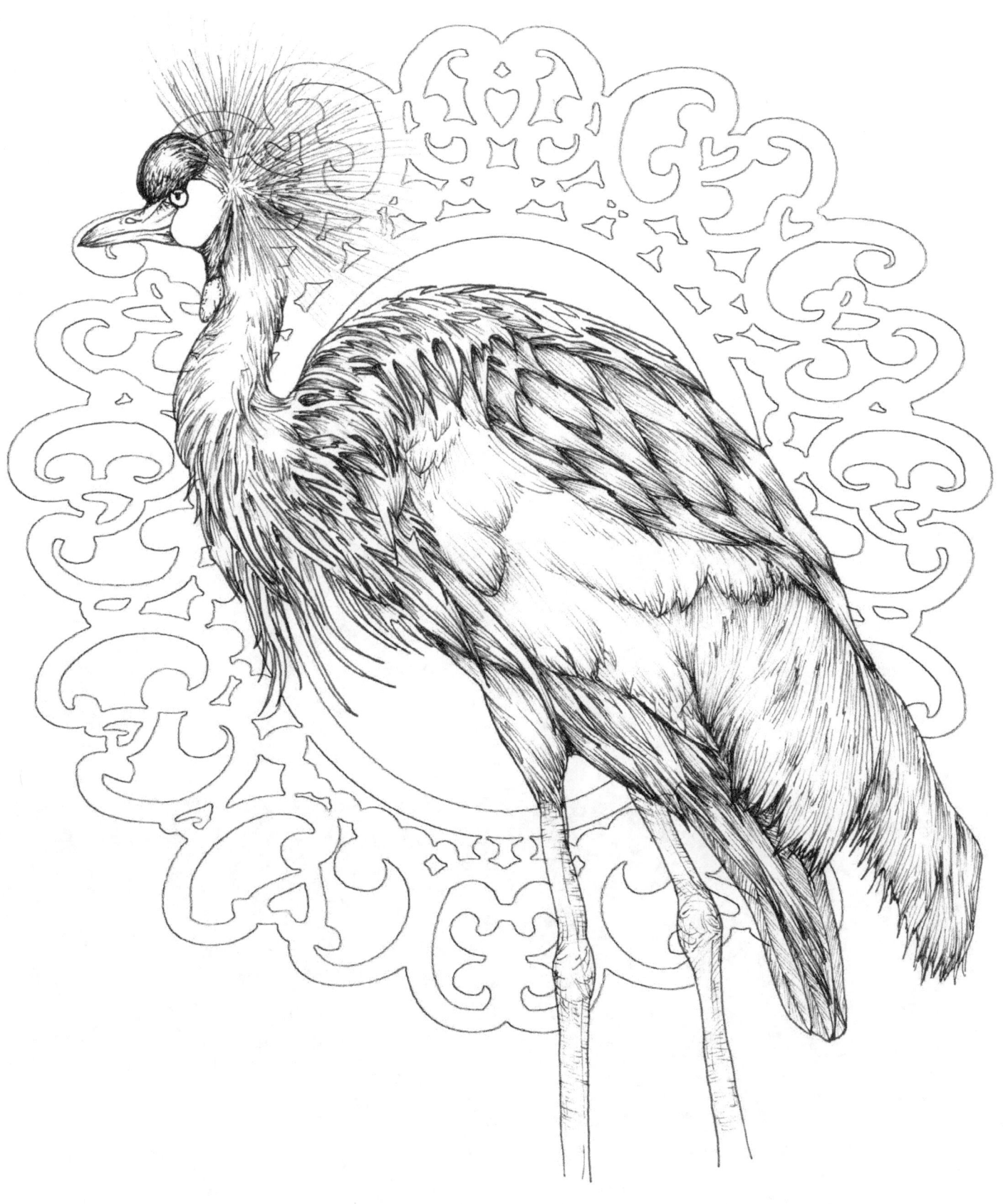

Casey Gilmore

COLOR LOG

THIS IS YOUR SPACE TO TEST COLOR SCHEMES AND LOG WHAT COLORS YOU USED FOR THE PAGES INSIDE THE BOOK. HAVE FUN AND EXPERIMENT !!

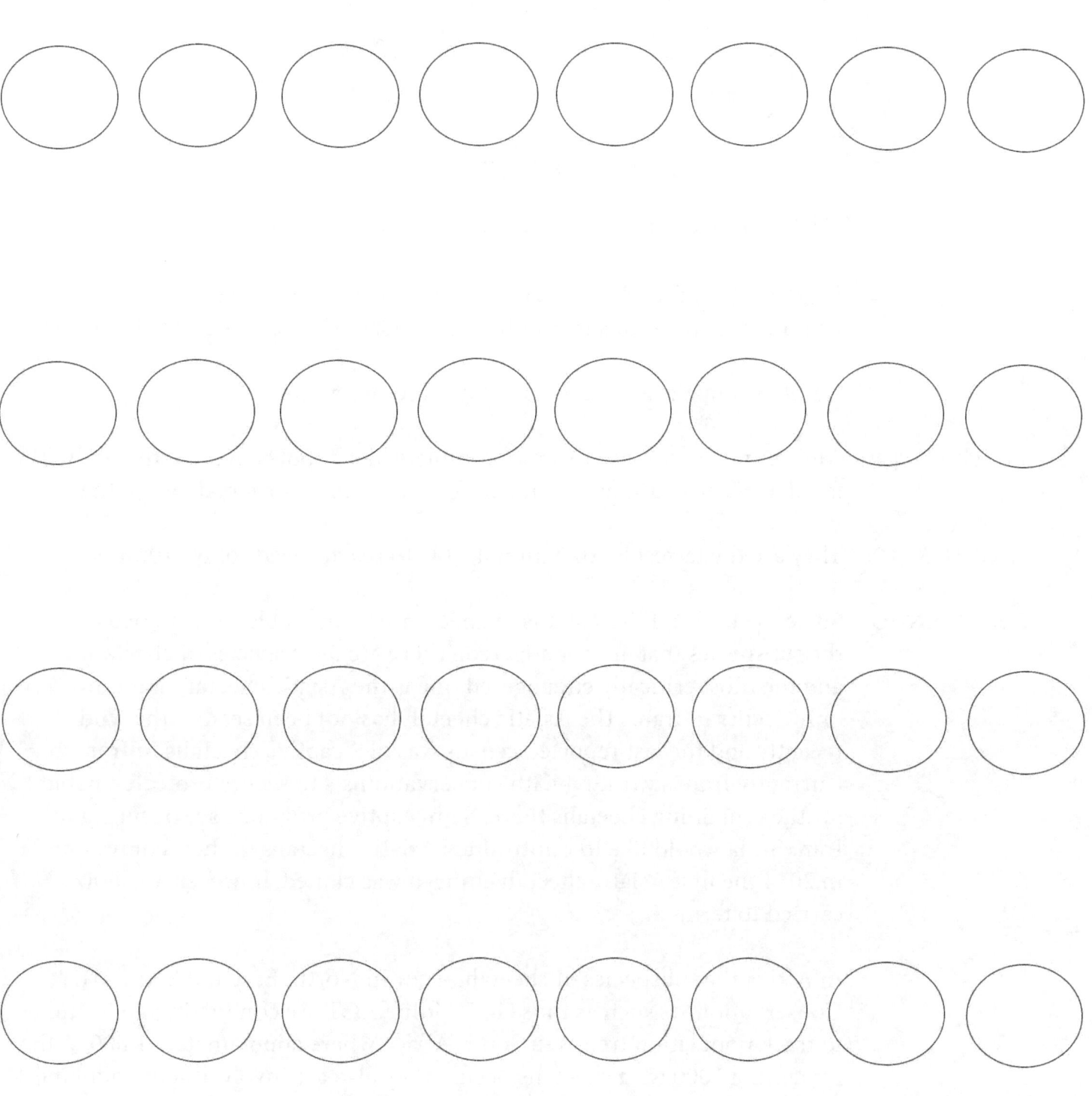

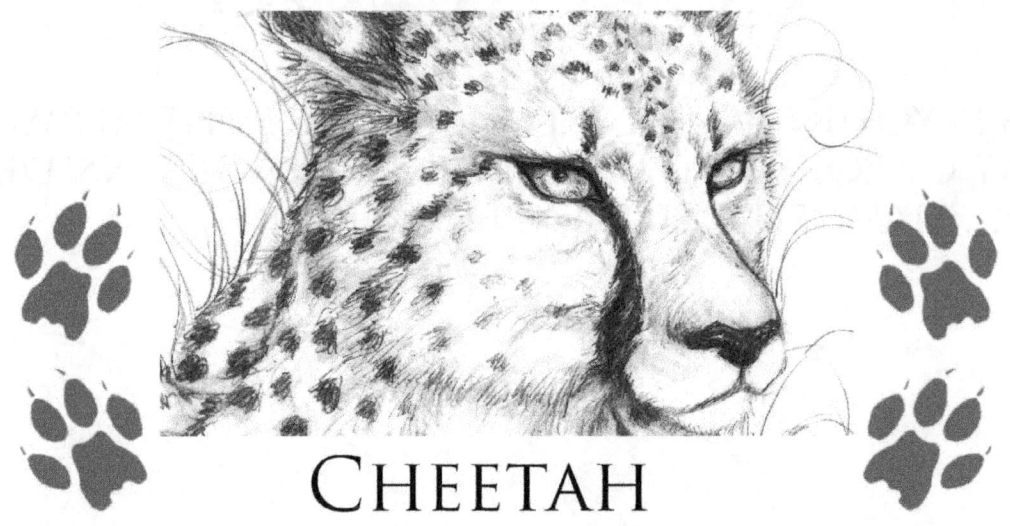

CHEETAH
SCIENTIFIC NAME: *ACINONYX JUBATUS*

HABITAT: In Africa they found in savannahs occuring in several countries with most populations in South Africa. Asian cheetahs occur only in Iran.

DIET: Gazelles, impala, and other small hooved mammals.

COLORATION: All over tawny color with small complete black spots covering the body. The face has black tear marks that run from the inner corners down to the jaw.

UNIQUENESS: They are the fastest land mammal, able to reach speeds of 60-70mph.

CONSERVATION: Since the overall IUCN status of cheetahs is vulnerable we will focus on the subspecies that are endangered. There are 5 subspecies of cheetah, and the most critically endangered one is the Asiatic cheetah that now only occurs in Iran. The Asiatic cheetah has not been seen in the wild recently and the last reported census was of 2 captive cheetahs in Iran. Currently Iran is working with conservationists to secure protected habitat for the remaining cheetahs there. Semi captive programs are occuring in Iran. India would like to reintroduce Asiatic cheetahs to their country and in 2014 the first Asiatic cheetah embryo was cloned, however was not carried to term.

In Africa the subspecies of cheetah occur in North, East and South Africa. Conservationists such as those in Wildlife ACT are conducting field studies to track population trends in South Africa where appoximately 1,000 of the remaining 7000 wild cheetahs occur. They also are involved reintroducing and transporting cheetahs to suitable habitats.

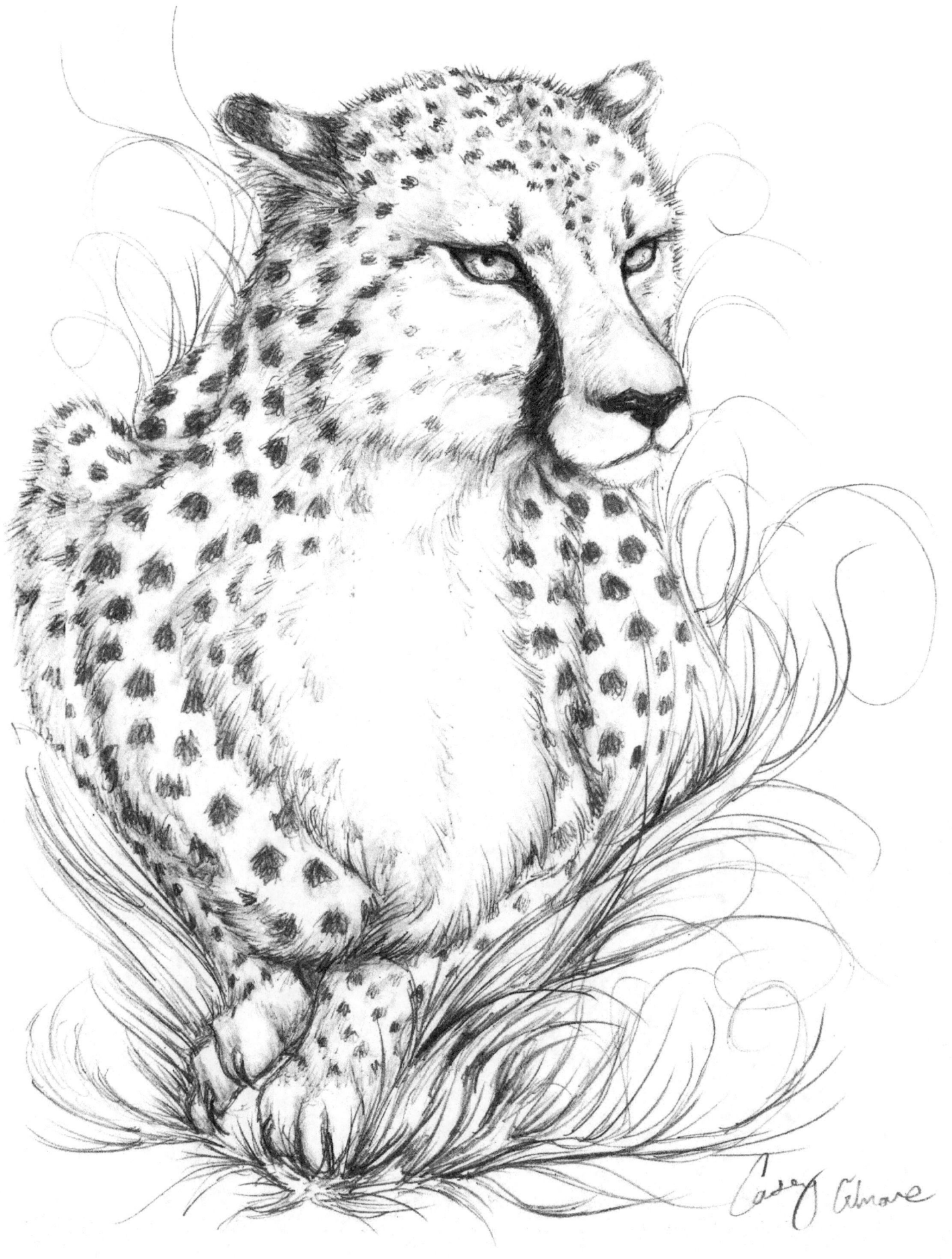

COLOR LOG

THIS IS YOUR SPACE TO TEST COLOR SCHEMES AND LOG
WHAT COLORS YOU USED FOR THE PAGES INSIDE THE
BOOK. HAVE FUN AND EXPERIMENT !!

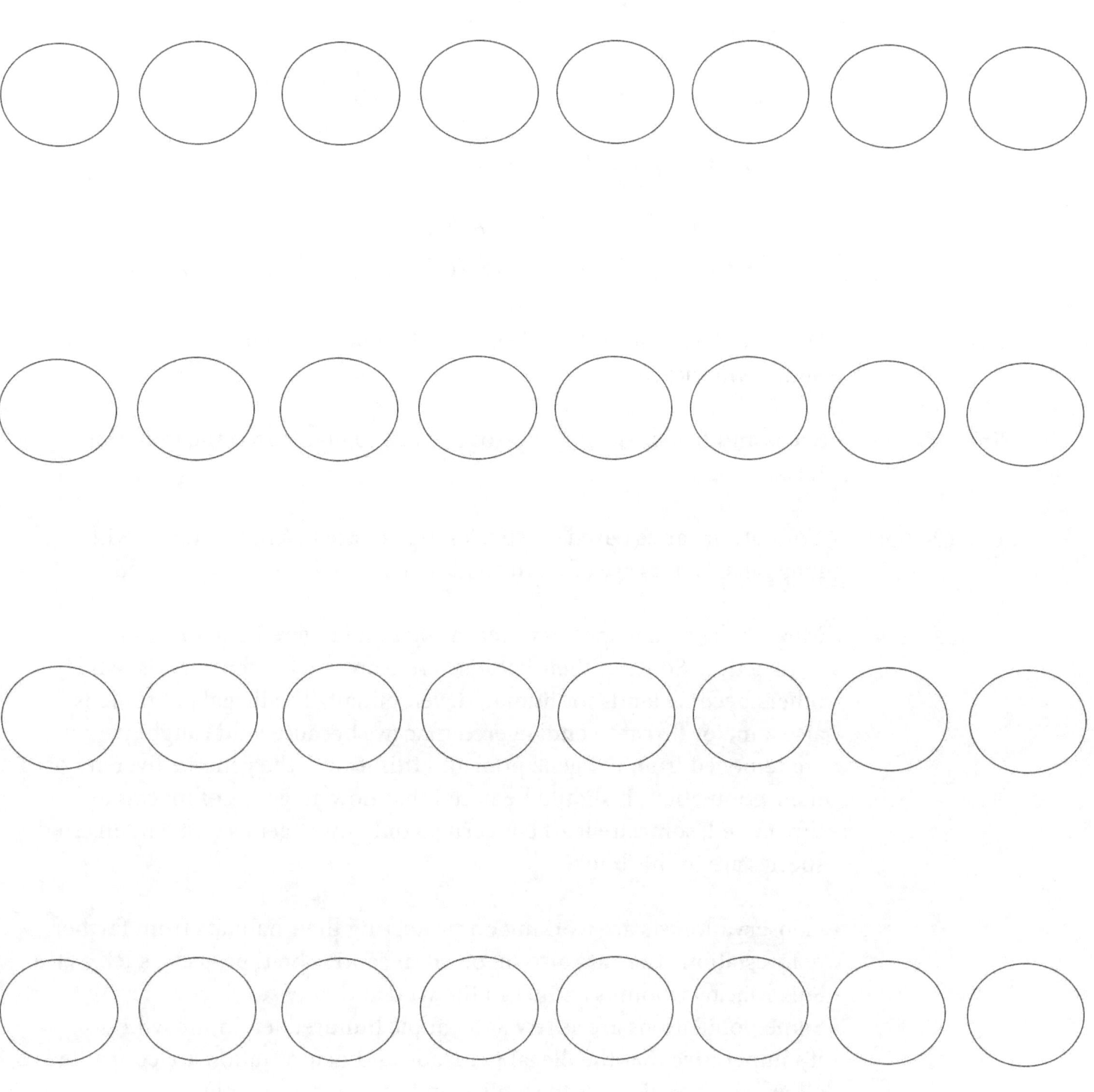

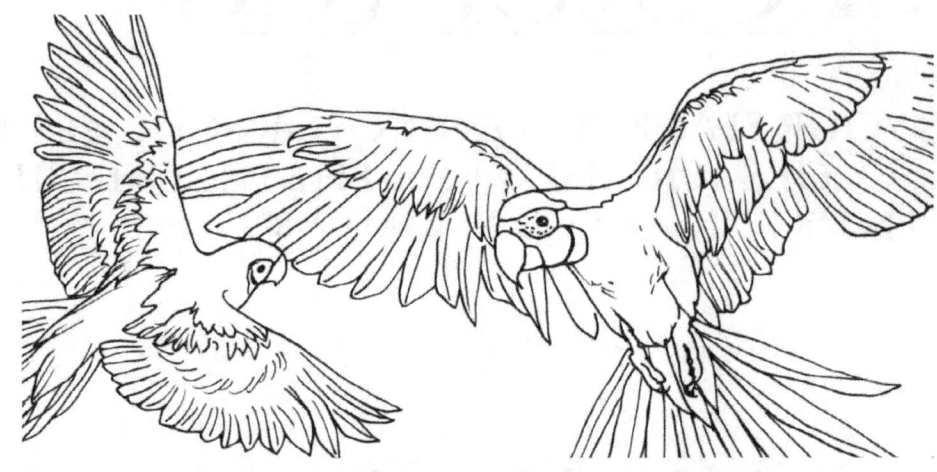

Macaw Species
Scientific Name:
Cyanopsitta, Ara, Anodorhynchus

HABITAT: Wet and dry rainforests and riparian habitats of Central and South America.

DIET: Seeds and fruits. They have strong beaks to break even the toughest husk.

COLORATION: Coloration varies based on species, but all are brightly colorful with long tails. Colors are often in shades of green, blue, yellow, or red.

CONSERVATION: Most of the extant species of macaw are endangered due to habitat destruction. Some of their habitats are converted to farm lands, while others become lands for human development. The illegal pet trade is also a major threat to endangered macaws because wild caught parrots are removed from the gene pool and this lowers the genetic diversity of their population. It should be noted that now all genus of macaw are threatened, some are least concern so only three genus with endangered species are in this book.

Conservationists are working on protecting their habitats from farther deforestation. They are also involved in captive bred projects, such as the Spix Macaw whom is extinct in the wild and only survives in captivity. Some populations are as few as a couple hundred left in the wild, so it's imperative that the illegal pet trade and deforestation are controlled to allow wild populations to stablize and increase over time.

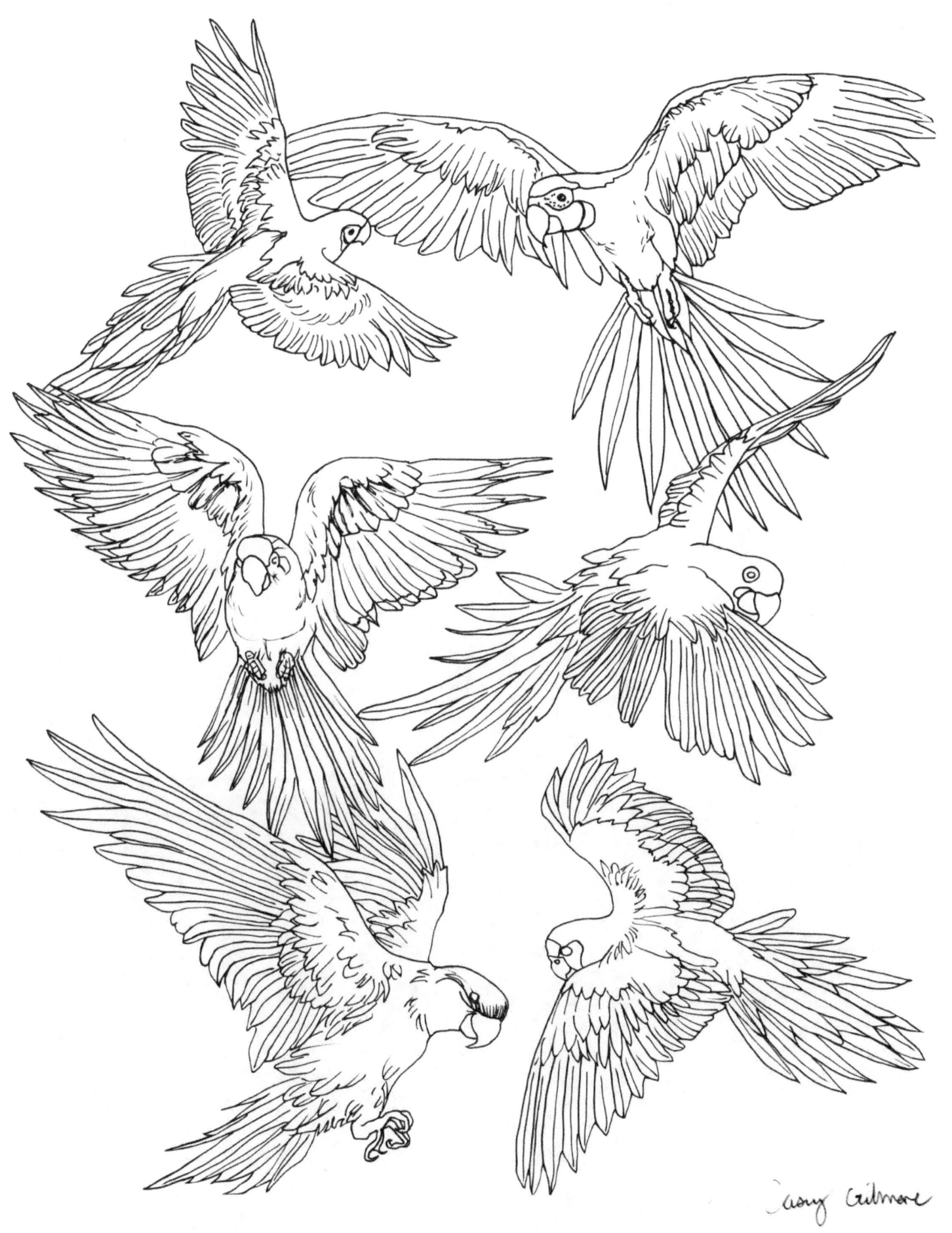

COLOR LOG

THIS IS YOUR SPACE TO TEST COLOR SCHEMES AND LOG
WHAT COLORS YOU USED FOR THE PAGES INSIDE THE
BOOK. HAVE FUN AND EXPERIMENT !!

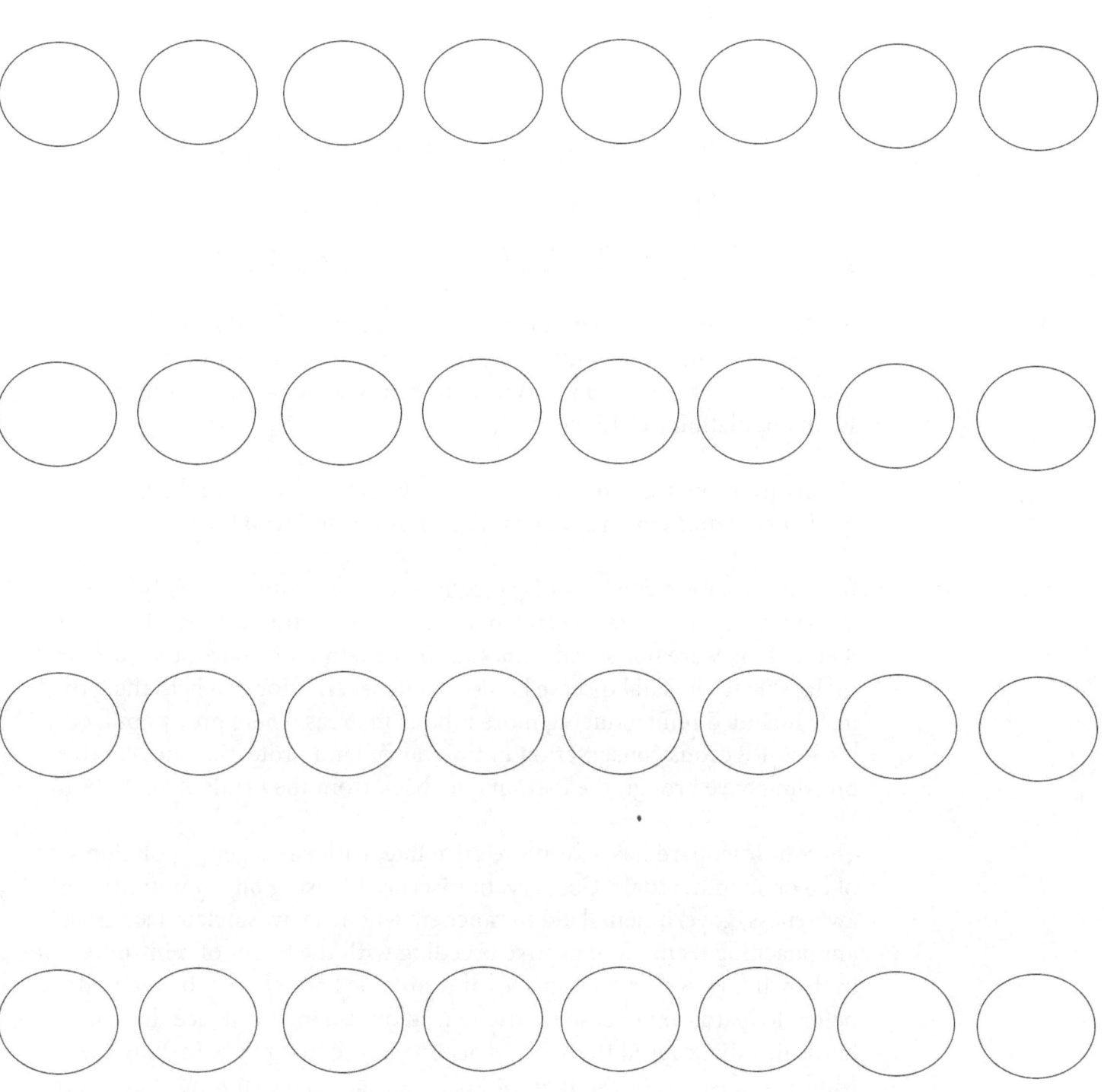

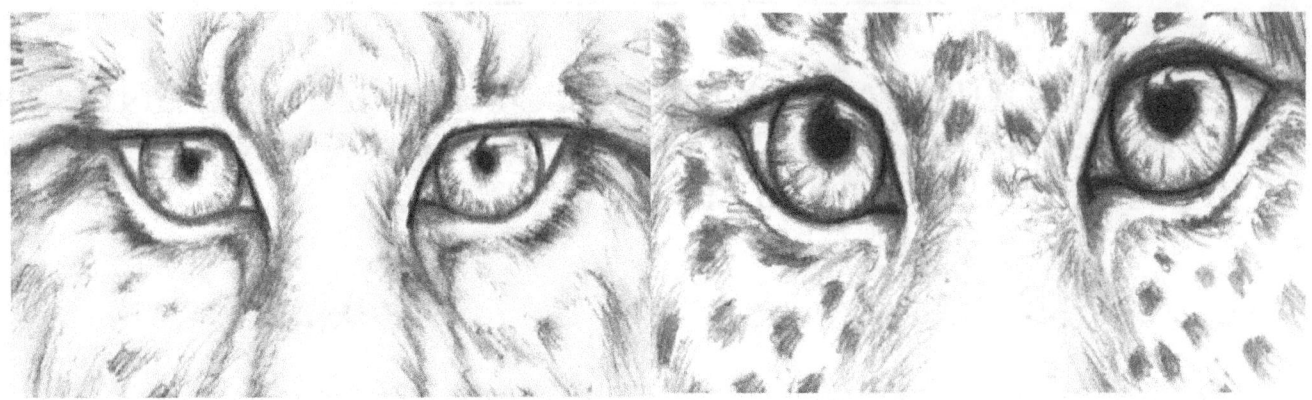

Iberian Lynx and Amur Leopard
Scientific Name: *Lynx pardinus*
Panthera pardus orientalis

Habitat: Iberian lynx are restricted to mountainous grassland and scrub lands of the Iberian Pennisula. While the amur leopard are found only in the cold forests of the Russian Province of Primorsky Krai, with perhaps a small population in China.

Diet: Carnivorous; iberian lynx are almost exclusively european rabbit predators. Amur leopard prey on deer, moose, and wild boar.

Conservation: Both species were considered critically endangered until recently when the iberian lynx was relisted as endangered. The main threats historically for iberian lynx were massive declines in their main food source the european rabbit due to the fatal disease hemorrhagic fever. Efforts to help the lynx have included reintroducing more rabbits to areas where prey populations are low. Rigorous conservation in the way of land protection and captive breeding have brough the iberian lynx back from the brink of extinction.

The Amur leopard has a far more grim fate, with a meager population size of 60 or so individuals. Conservationists are focusing on community awareness, governmental aid to ranchers who lose livestock to leopards, antipoaching teams, and captive breeding with the hopes of reintroduction in the wild. However prey species and suitable habitat must be secured before leopards are released into the wild or else they will face the same hardships that caused the species' decline in the first place. In 2009 the Ministry of Natural Resources of Russia announced that funds have been put aside for land with suitable and safe habitat for the leopards.

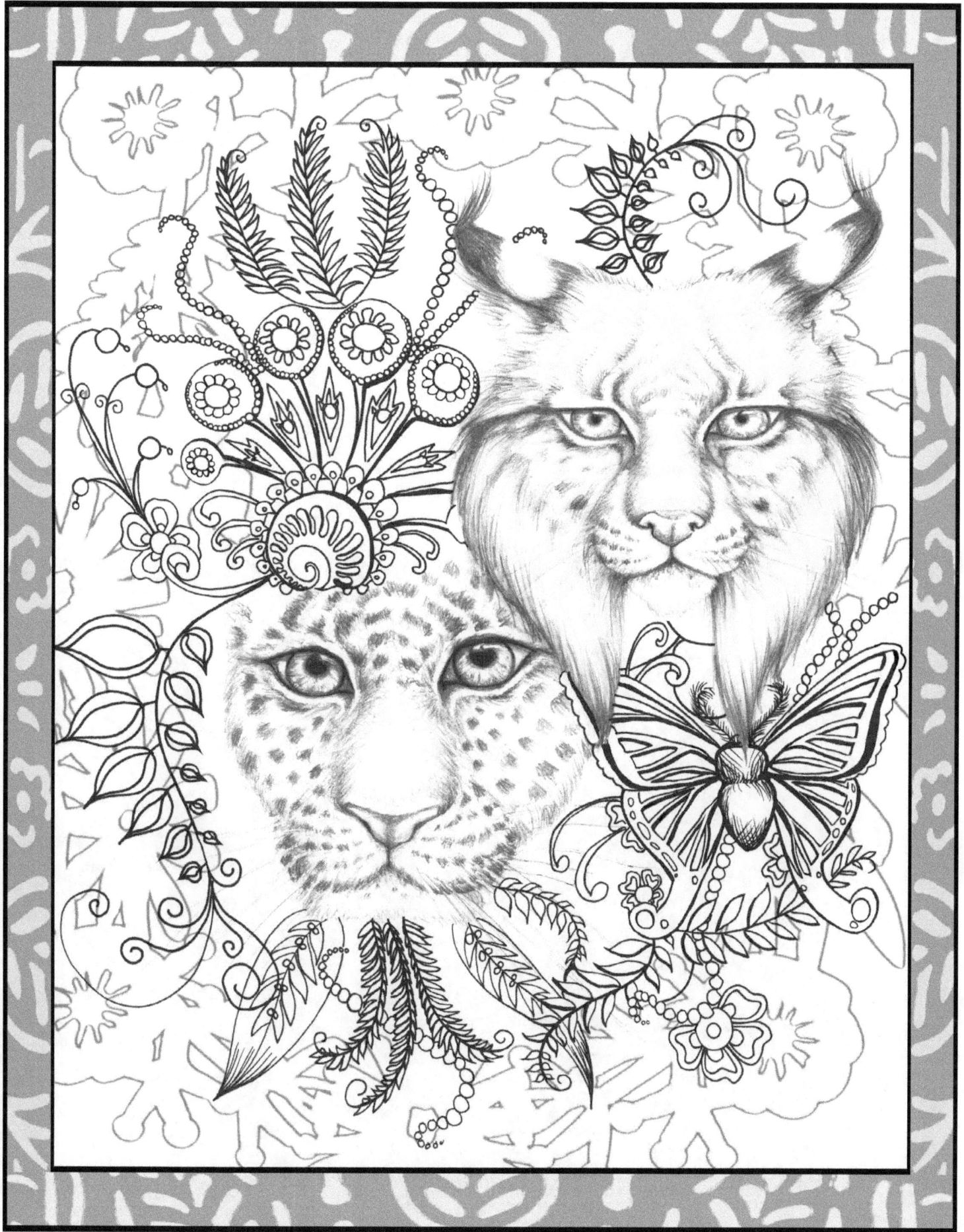

COLOR LOG

THIS IS YOUR SPACE TO TEST COLOR SCHEMES AND LOG
WHAT COLORS YOU USED FOR THE PAGES INSIDE THE
BOOK. HAVE FUN AND EXPERIMENT !!

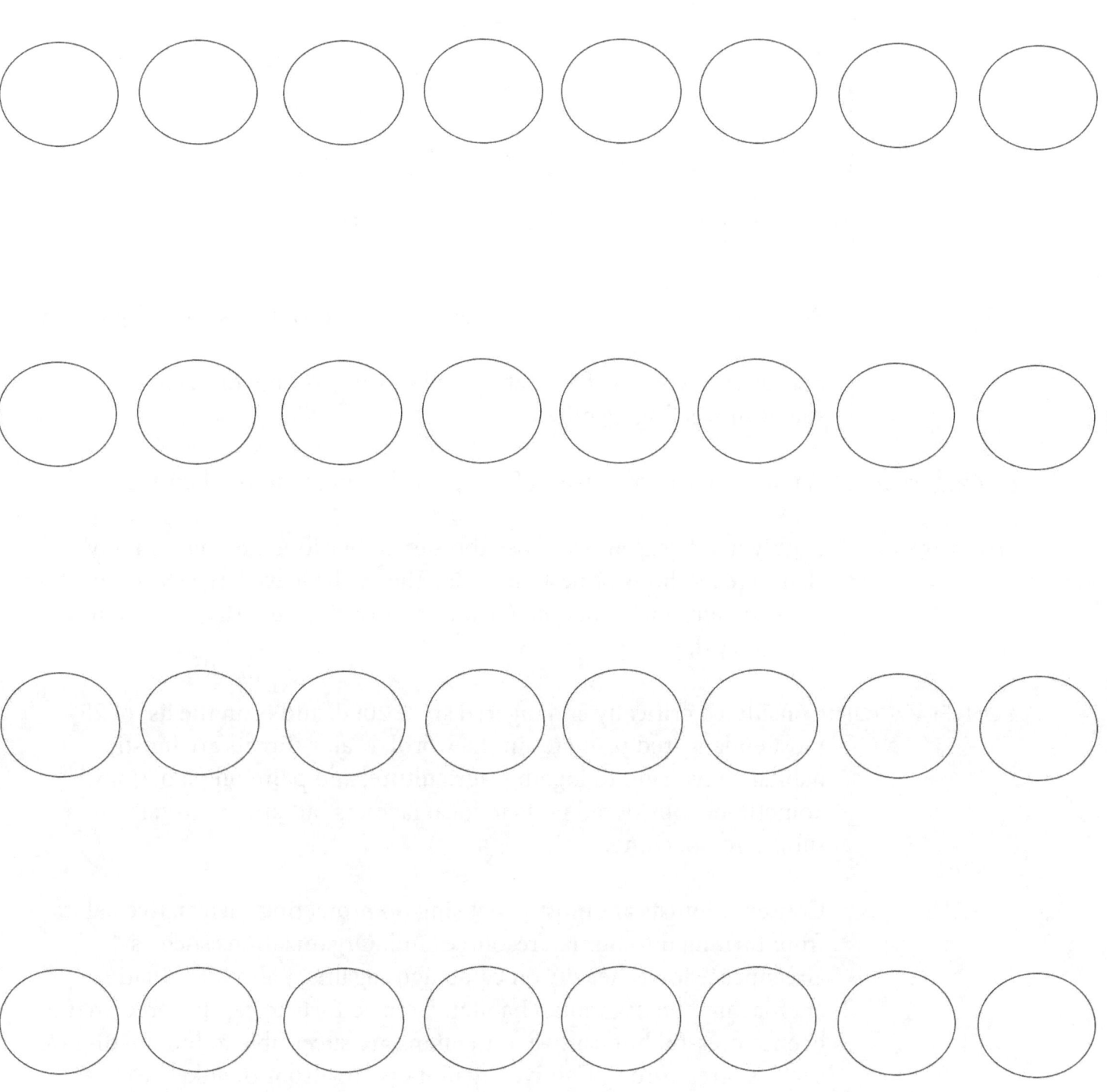

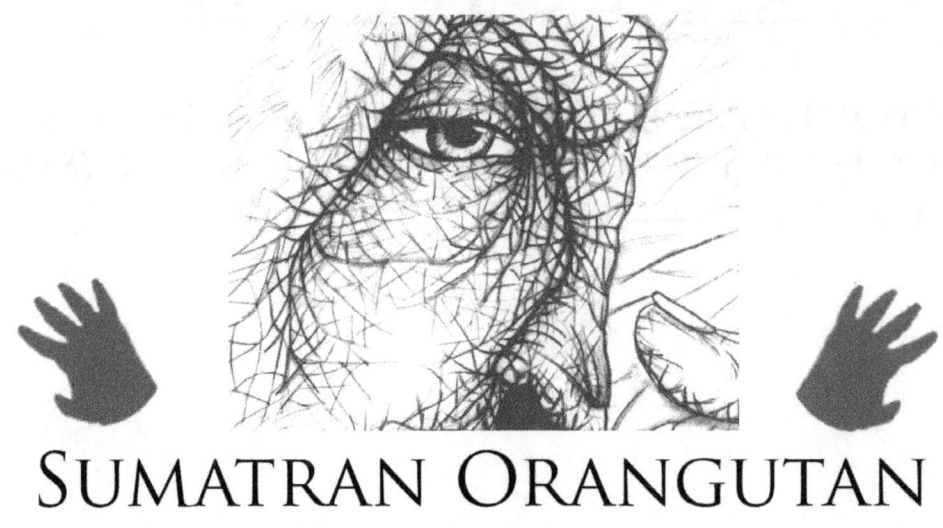

SUMATRAN ORANGUTAN
SCIENTIFIC NAME: PONGO ABELII

HABITAT: Restricted to the northern tropical rain forests of the island of Sumatra.

DIET: Mainly frugivorous (fruit eating) with some insectivorous behavior sometimes eating termites.

COLORATION: Coppery red all over with bluish gray skin pigment on their face.

UNIQUENESS: Highly intelligent and will use tools to gather food and have highly elaborate methods of nest building. They will weave large leaves together to form hammocks that hang from trees to sleep in. They build a new nest every day.

CONSERVATION: Considered critically endangered since 2000, and is on the list of 25 most endangered primates in the world. Major threats are mostly habitat conversion to logging, agriculture, and palm oil planations. Sometimes considered pests to local farmers but are not usually subject to poaching.

Conservationists are mostly focusing on protecting their native habitat from turning into human resource land. Organizations such as Greenpeace focus heavily on campaigns against palm oil planations encroaching on organutan habitat. Some efforts to captive breed have been successful but captive orangutans are suceptible to human diseases such as Strep throat. Captive organutans are also more likely to lose the skills needed to survive in the wild if in captivity to long.

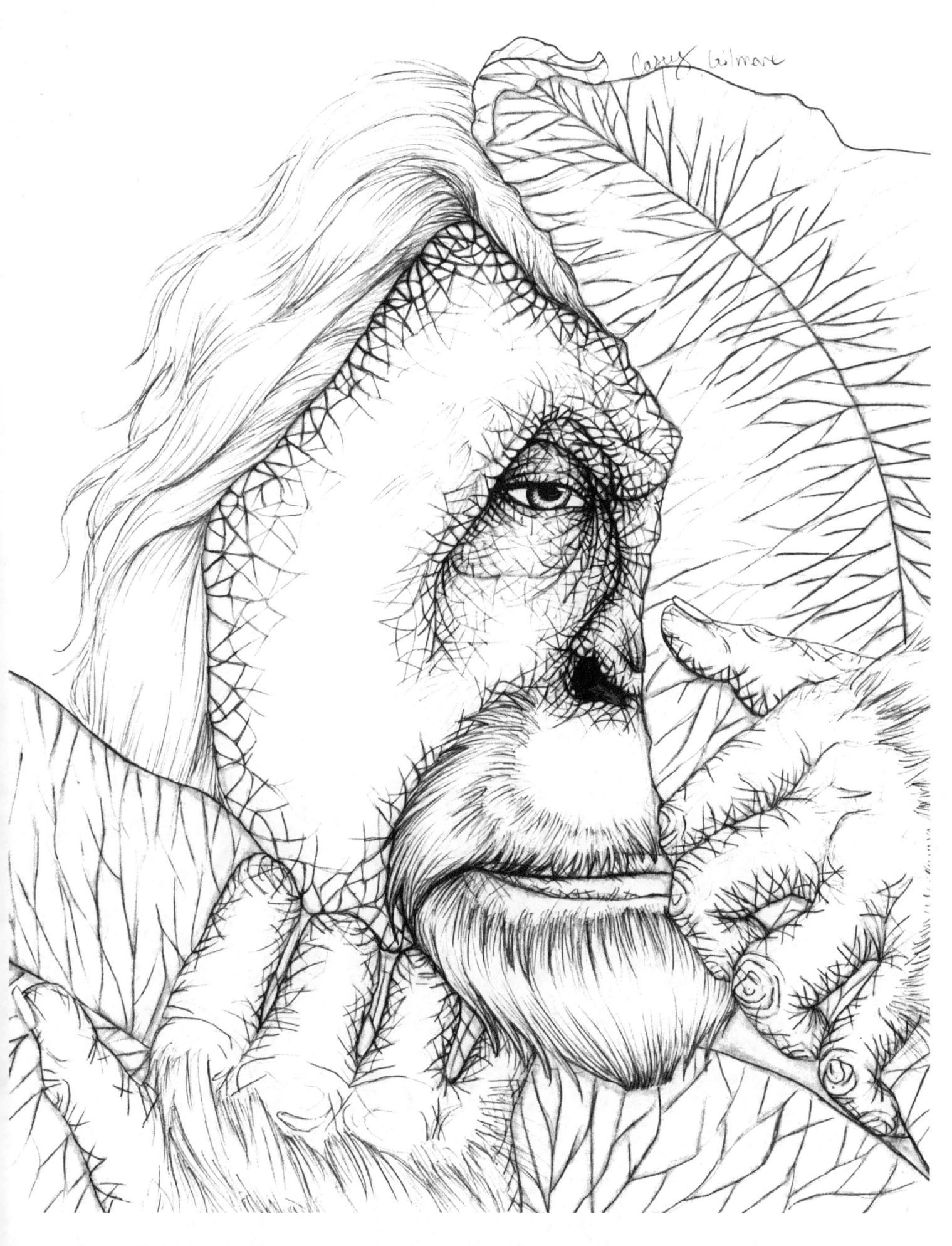

COLOR LOG

THIS IS YOUR SPACE TO TEST COLOR SCHEMES AND LOG
WHAT COLORS YOU USED FOR THE PAGES INSIDE THE
BOOK. HAVE FUN AND EXPERIMENT !!

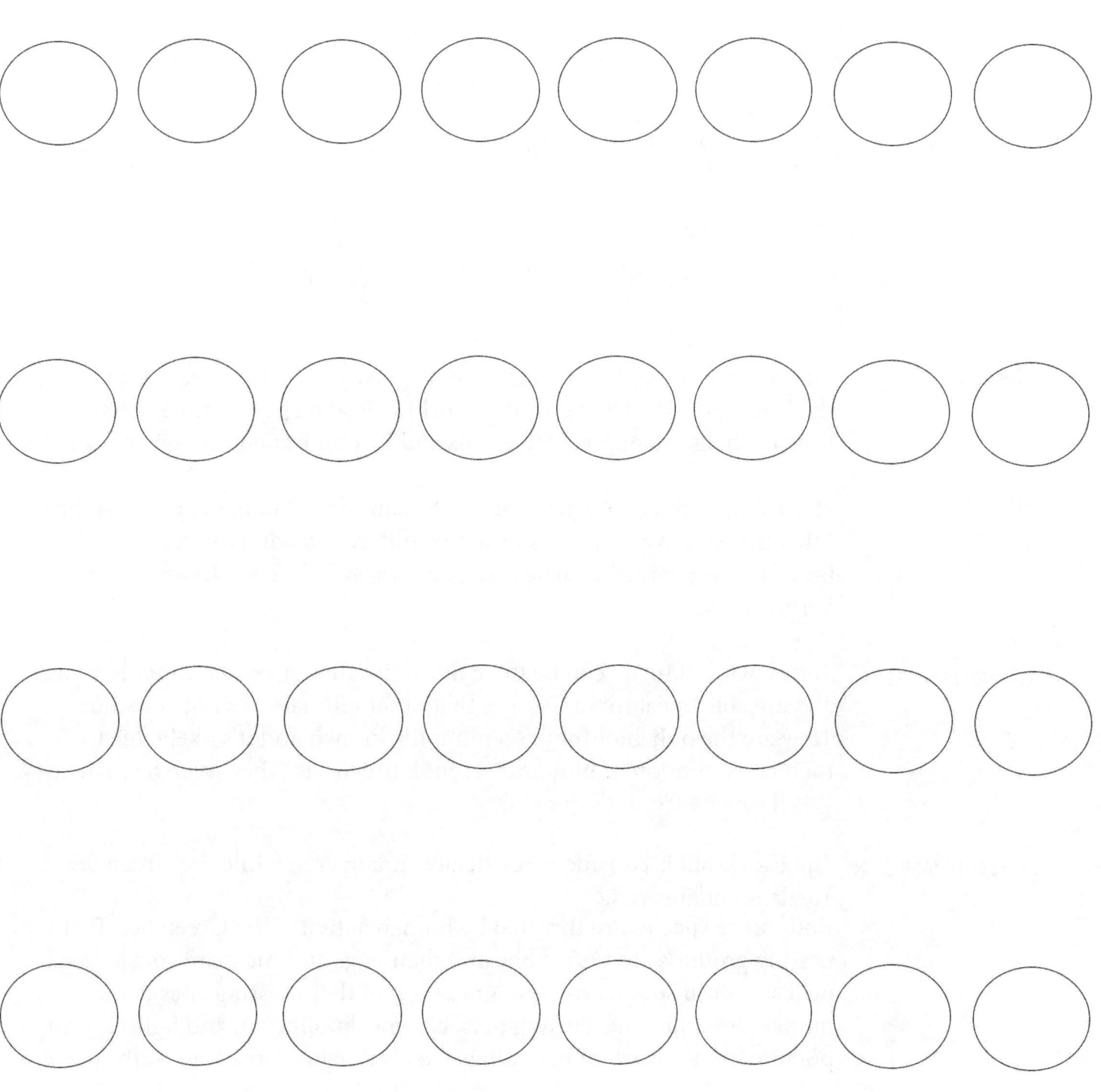

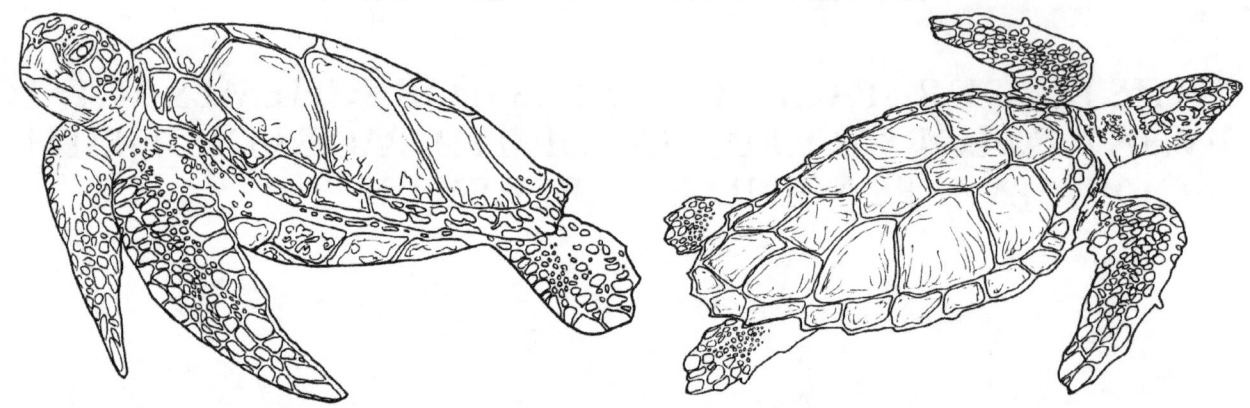

GREEN & HAWKSBILL SEA TURTLES

SCIENTIFIC NAME: *CHELONIS MYDAS* AND *ERETMOCHELYS IMBRICATA*

HABITAT: The Green Sea Turtle inhabitats subtropical and tropical waters, while the Hawksbill Sea Turtle is more worldwide and spends most of its time in shallow lagoons with corals and less time spent in open ocean.

DIET: Hawksbill feed on sponges and crustaceans found in the coral reefs they inhabitat. Green Sea Turtles have two different feeding preferences based on age; younger turtles are omnivorous while adults are herbivorous.

UNIQUENESS: The Hawksbill turtle can be toxic due to it's diet of vemonous cnidarians, and are able to eat toxic sponges that other animals can not consume. They are the only bioluminescent reptile known and it's likely due to their consumption of bioluminescent hard corals. The Green Sea Turtle gets it's name from it's green fat.

CONSERVATION: The Hawksbill is considered critically endangered while the Green Sea Turtle is endangered.
Both turtle species are threated by human activity. The Green Sea Turtle's nesting grounds are raided because their eggs and meat are considered a delicacy. Both species suffer degradation of their nesting sites from human development. Fishing nets, chemical pollution, and light pollution that disorient hatchlings are also major threats for both species.

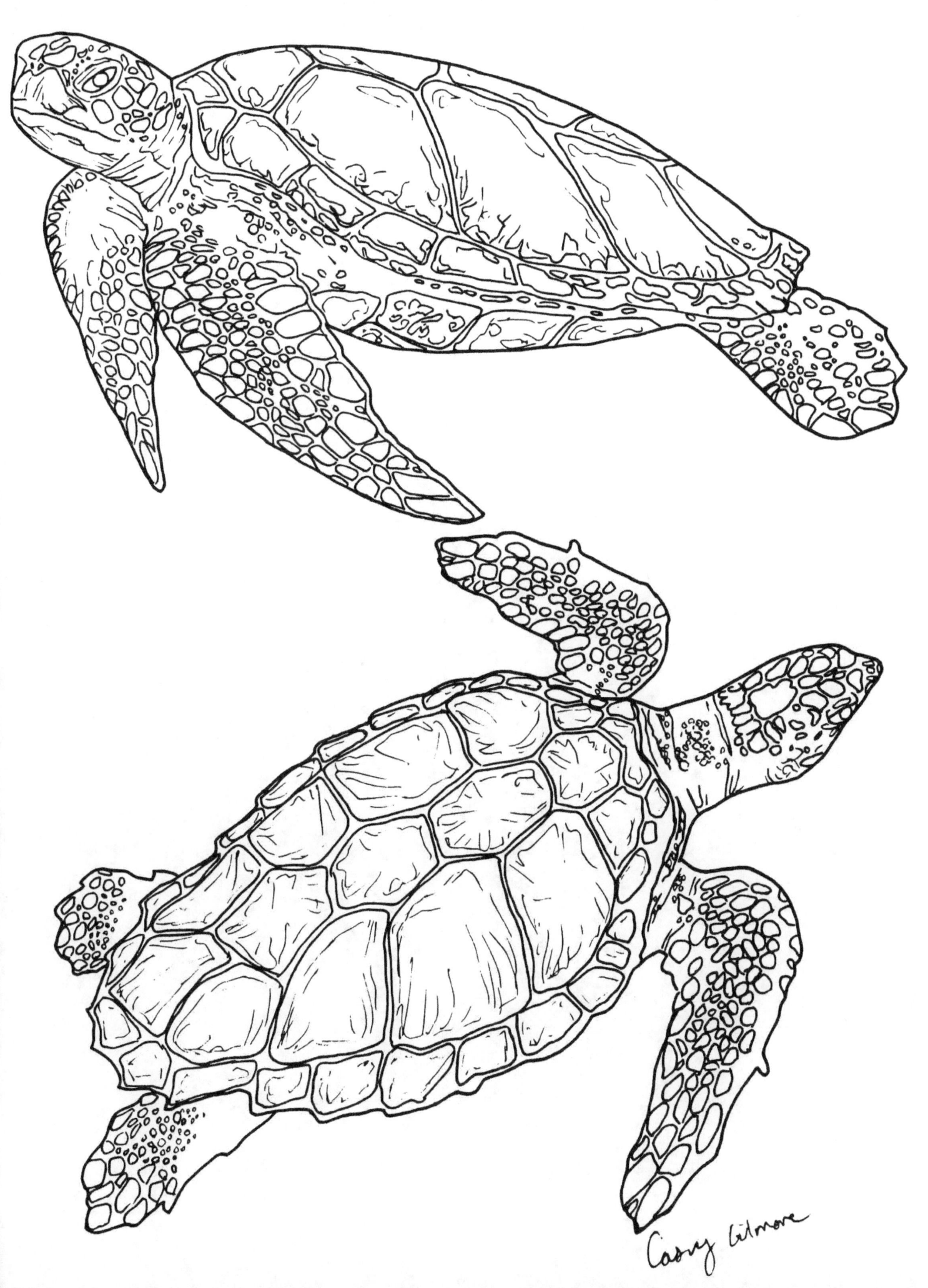

Casey Gilmore

COLOR LOG

THIS IS YOUR SPACE TO TEST COLOR SCHEMES AND LOG WHAT COLORS YOU USED FOR THE PAGES INSIDE THE BOOK. HAVE FUN AND EXPERIMENT !!

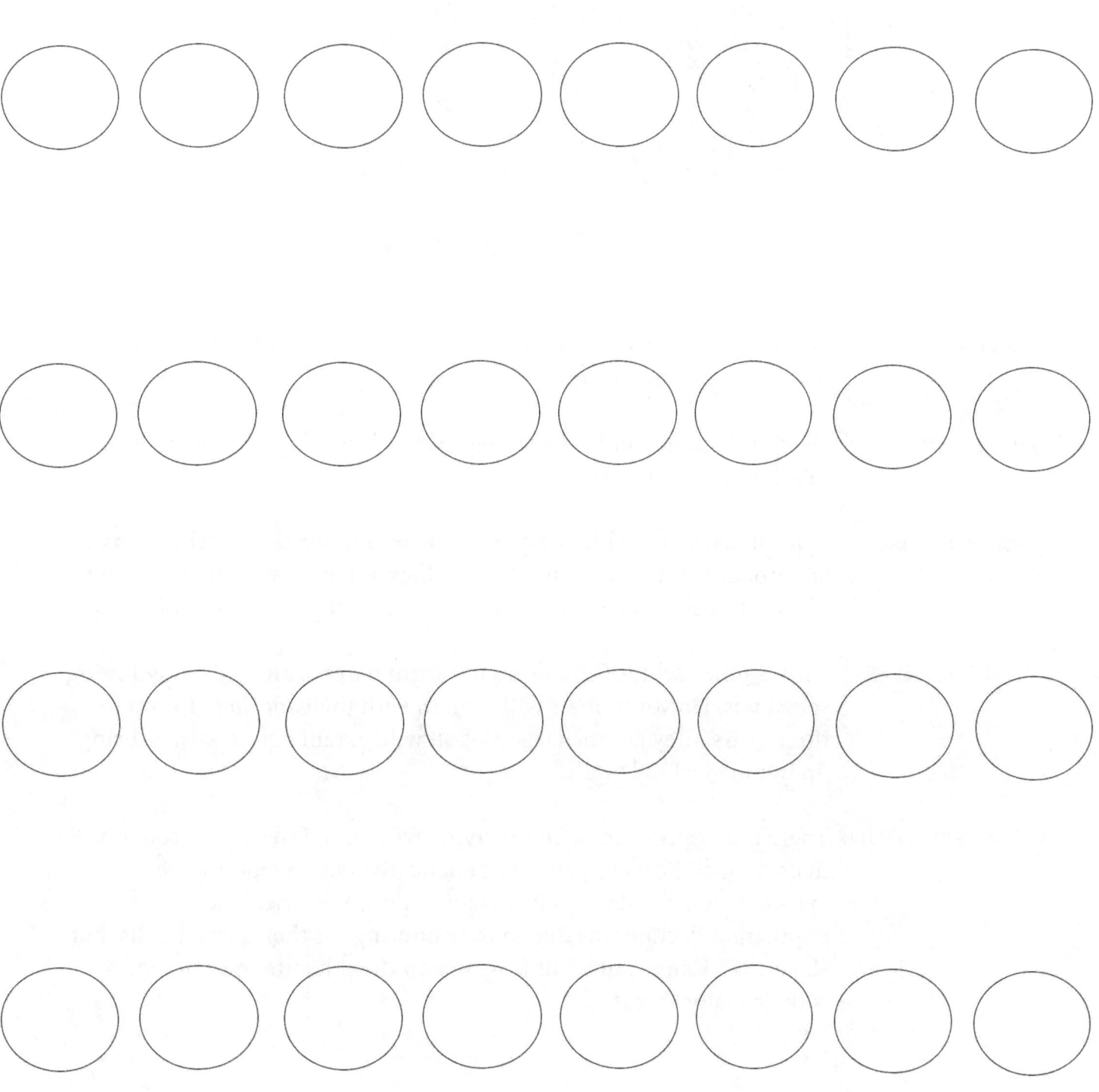

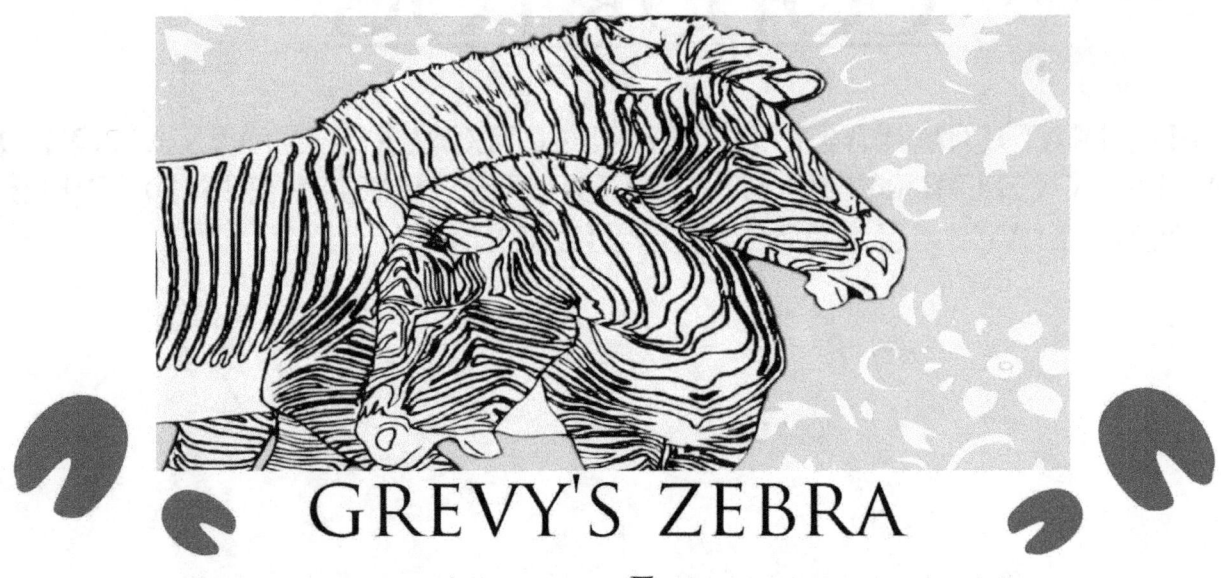

GREVY'S ZEBRA

SCIENTIFIC NAME: *EQUUS GREVYI*

HABITAT: Occupies semi-arid bushlands and barren plains of Northern Kenya with smaller populations in Ethiopia.

DIET: Grasses, legumes and other foliage while browsing. Can survive up to five days without water.

COLORATION: Typical black and white striping as seen in other zebras. The strips are broader on the neck and thin as they extend down the legs and back The underbelly and around the tail are uniquely white without strips.

UNIQUENESS: Unlike other zebras Grevy's do not form harems and lack long lasting social ties. However, foals will remain with their mothers for up to three years. They are the largest of all wild extant equines, measuring up to nine feet in length.

CONSERVATION: There is an estimated 3000 surviving wild individuals with roughly 300 in captivity. Efforts to preserve genetic diversity include semen cyropreserving and artificial insemination. Historically their population decline was due to over hunting for their prized pelts, but since 1977 Kenya put a hunting ban on them habitat destruction is their major threat.

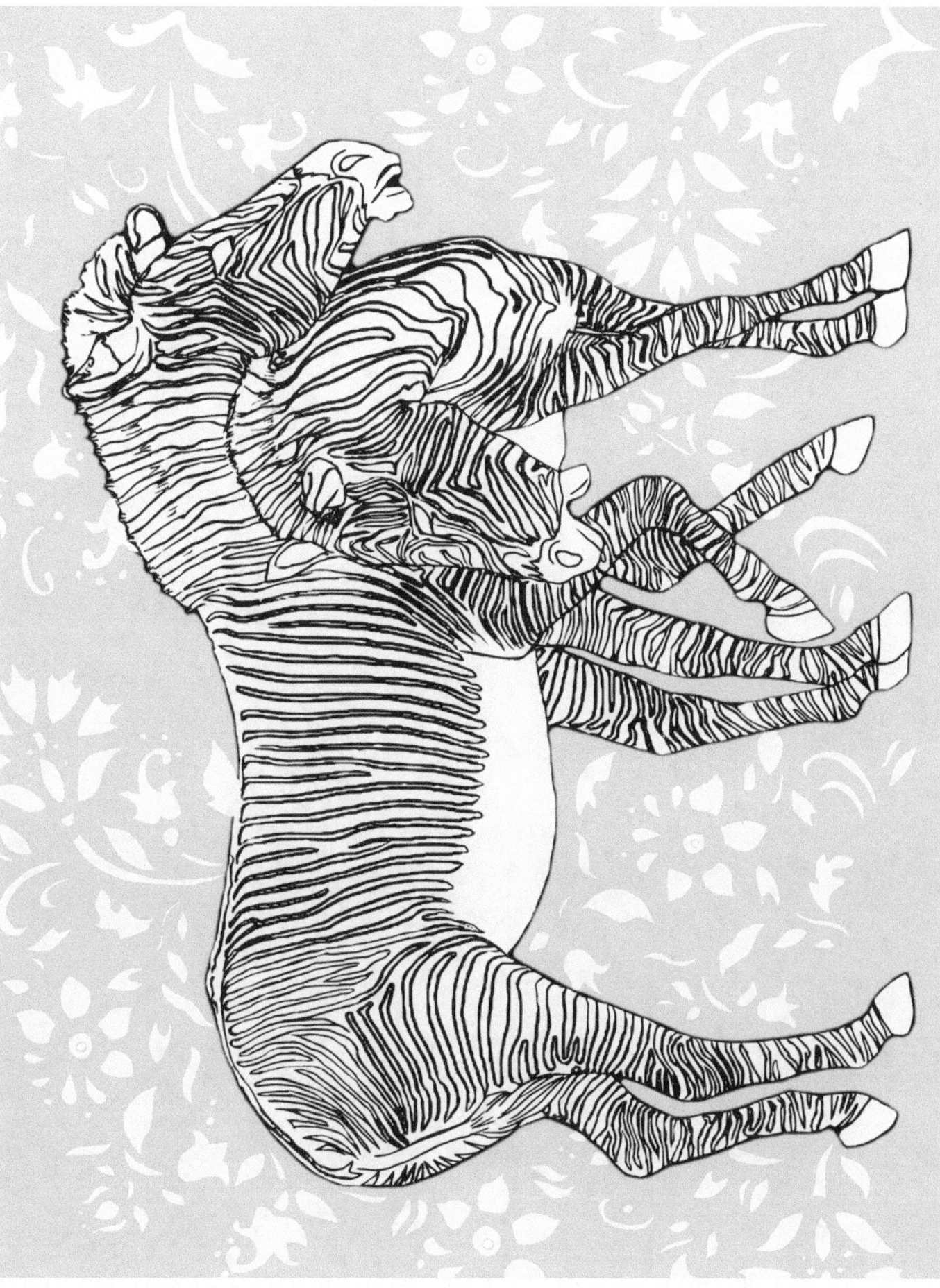

COLOR LOG

THIS IS YOUR SPACE TO TEST COLOR SCHEMES AND LOG
WHAT COLORS YOU USED FOR THE PAGES INSIDE THE
BOOK. HAVE FUN AND EXPERIMENT !!

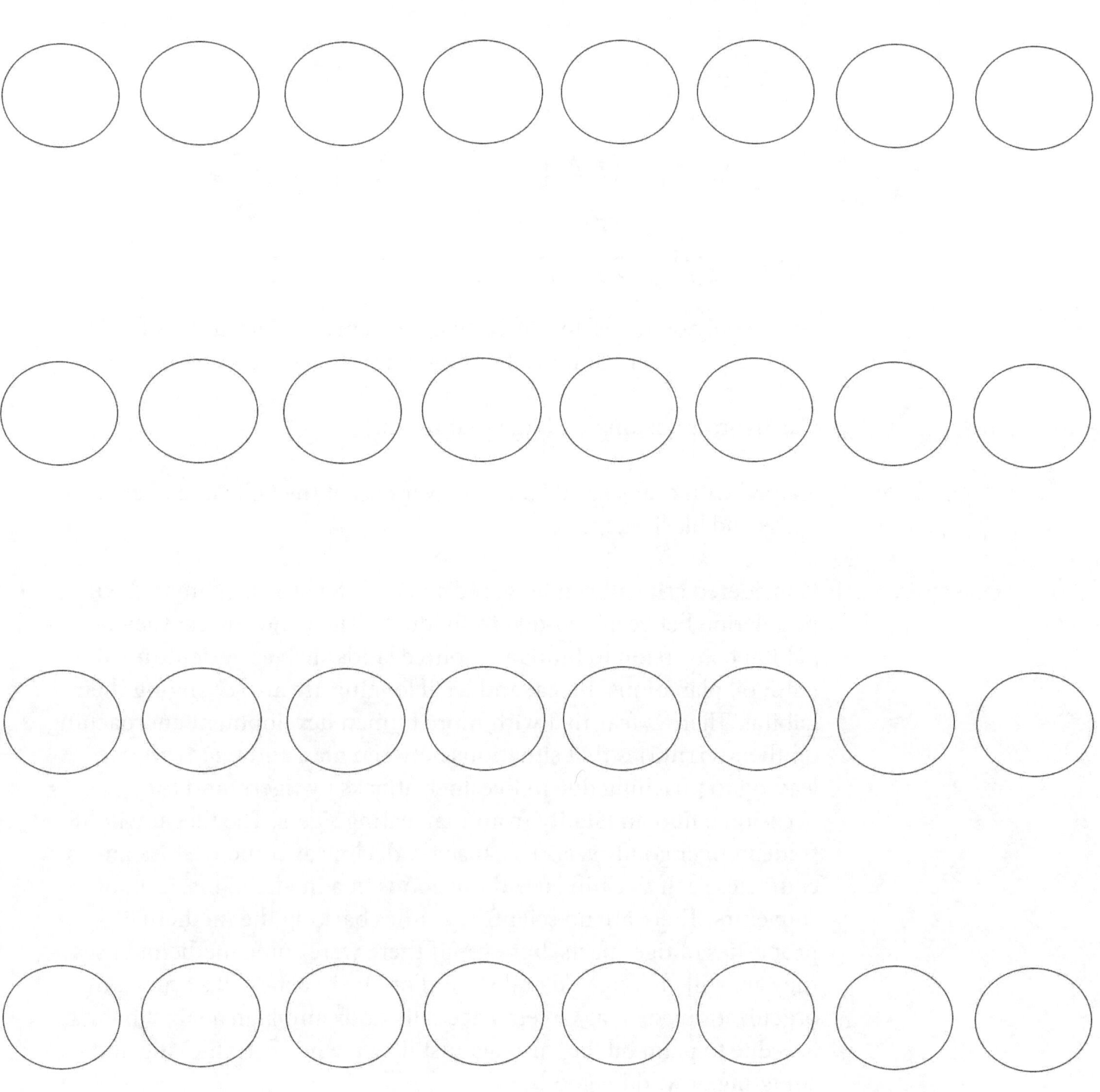

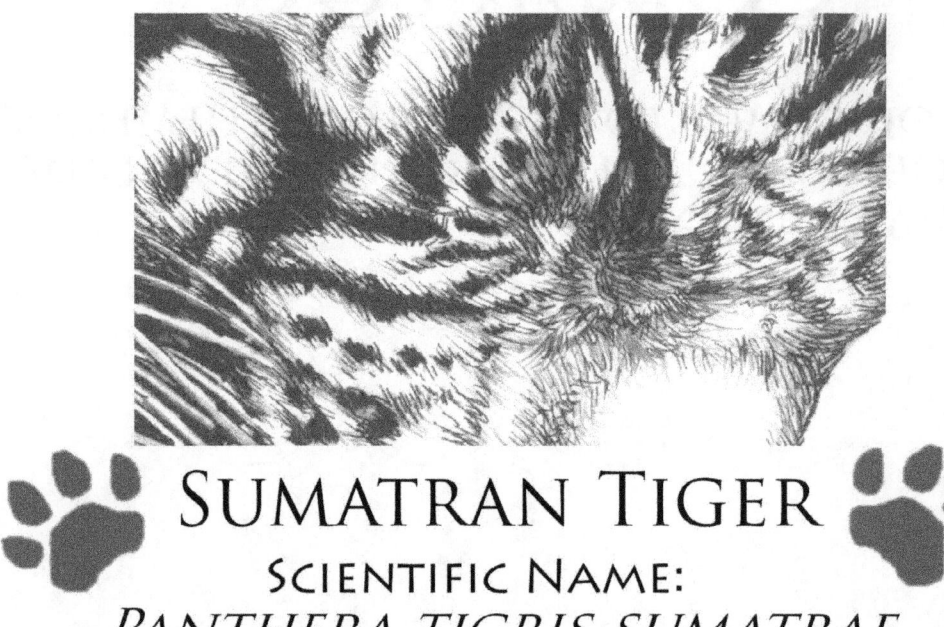

SUMATRAN TIGER
SCIENTIFIC NAME:
PANTHERA TIGRIS SUMATRAE

HABITAT: Found only on the island of Sumatra. Occuring in a variety of habitats from sea level coastal forests to mountain forests well above 8,000ft.

DIET: Carnivorous feeding on large mammals.

COLORATION: Striped with orange and black all over except the belly and chest with white and black stripes.

CONSERVATION: Considered critically endangered since 2008 with an estimated wild population between 400-600 individuals. The major threat they face is habitat conversion to human resource lands such as agriculture and palm oil planations. Illegal and legal logging are also changing their habitat. There is fear that with more human development encroaching on their territories that situations between man and tiger will rise leading to poaching due to livestock attacks by tigers, and the occasional human fatality from man eating tigers. The illegal wildlife trade in tiger goods is also a cause for decline as some East Asian countries such as China use these goods in a medicinal fashion or as souvenirs. There are no scientific studies backing the medicinal properties of tiger parts, but even if there were some medicinal uses they are still endangered and should not be poached. It's crucial that organizations such as Greenpeace rally and campaign against habitat loss due to palm oil, but also against illegal wildlife trafficking and smugling of wildlife goods.

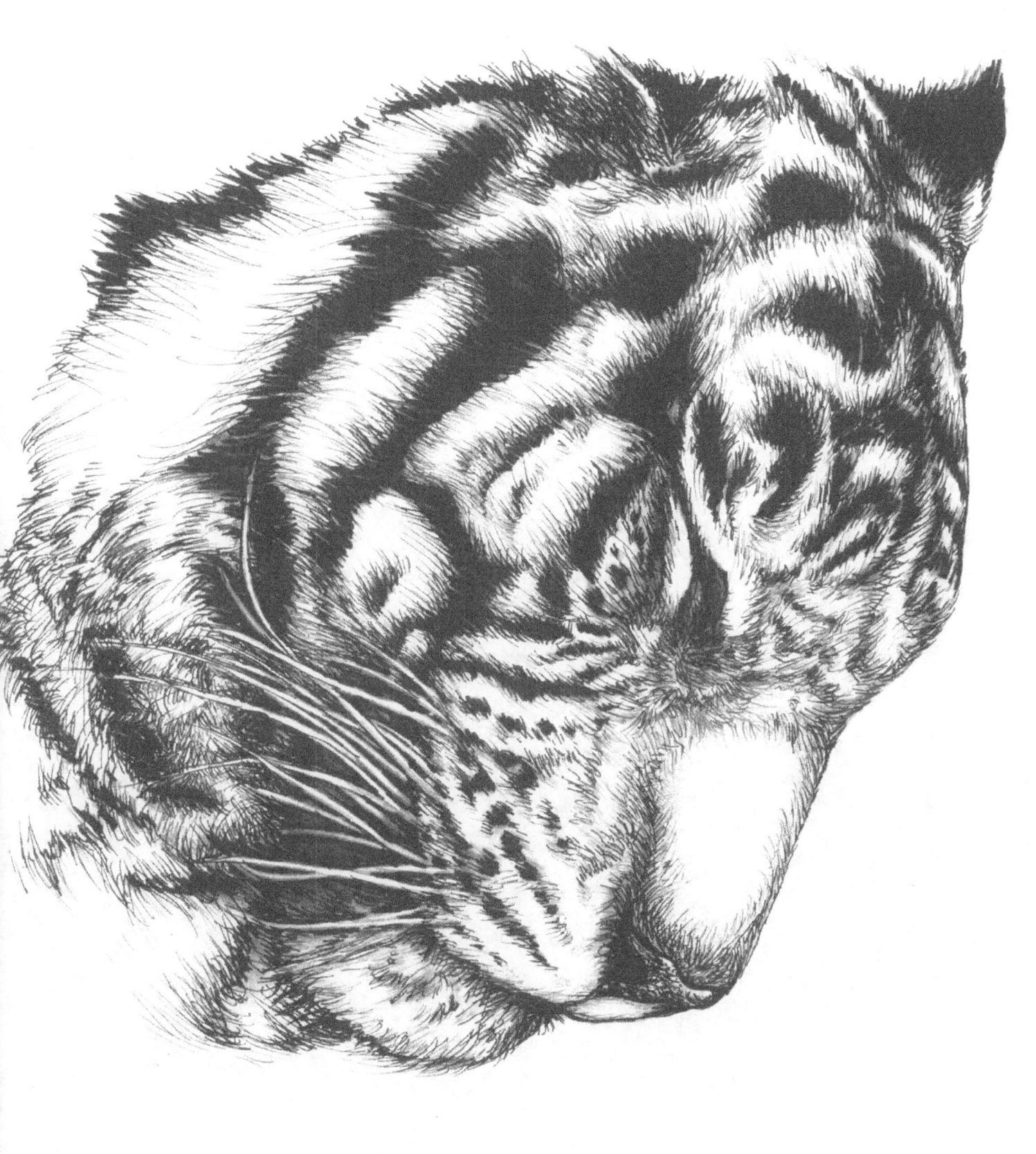

COLOR LOG

THIS IS YOUR SPACE TO TEST COLOR SCHEMES AND LOG
WHAT COLORS YOU USED FOR THE PAGES INSIDE THE
BOOK. HAVE FUN AND EXPERIMENT !!

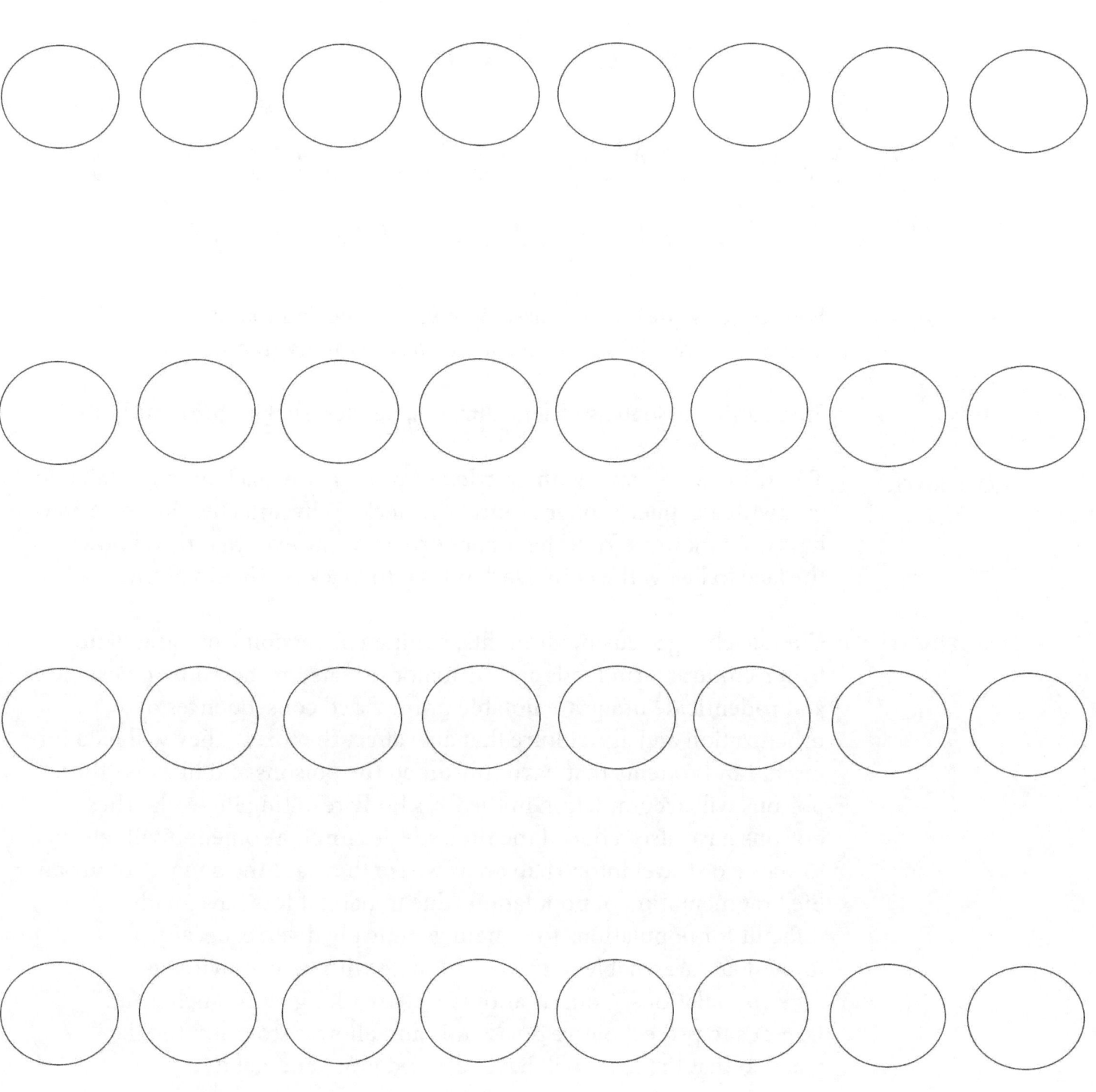

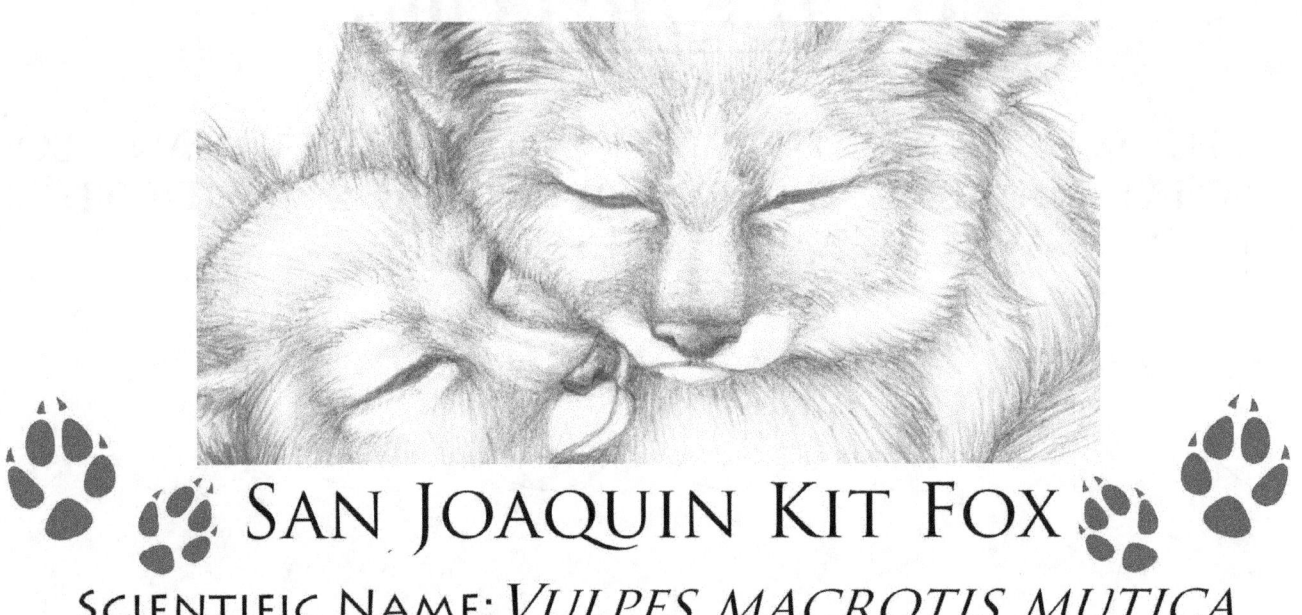

San Joaquin Kit Fox

Scientific Name: *Vulpes macrotis mutica*

HABITAT: Found along the native grassland edges of the San Joaquin Valley area of Central California. Populations are highly fragmented.

DIET: Small animals such as rodents, lizards, beetles, snakes, birds and rabbits.

COLORATION: Tawny brown all over with grizzled gray along the back onto the tail and face with a coppery collar around the neck. Belly and chest are pale. Face has two dark lines from the inner corners of the eyes that travel down the face to below the chin. Dark brown to black on the tip of their tail.

CONSERVATION: Climate change causing droughts, habitat conversion from grasslands to agricultural farm lands are the major threats for these foxes. Pesticide and rodenticide usage are notable unintended consequences of urbanization and agriculture that also affect the foxes. They will feed on insects and rodents that have consumed the poisons and likewise these poisons will accumulation in the fox's body resulting in death. These poisons have also reduced the prey species forcing some individuals to starve or travel into urban areas where they face the dangers of urban life.Fragmentation of populations due to habitat loss have made it difficult for populations to remain genetically diverse, because individuals are unable to travel and mate with new individuals in other populations. Conservationists are working with ranchers and farmer's to protect native grasslands and allow restoration to take place so that the foxes will have restored grassland habitat.

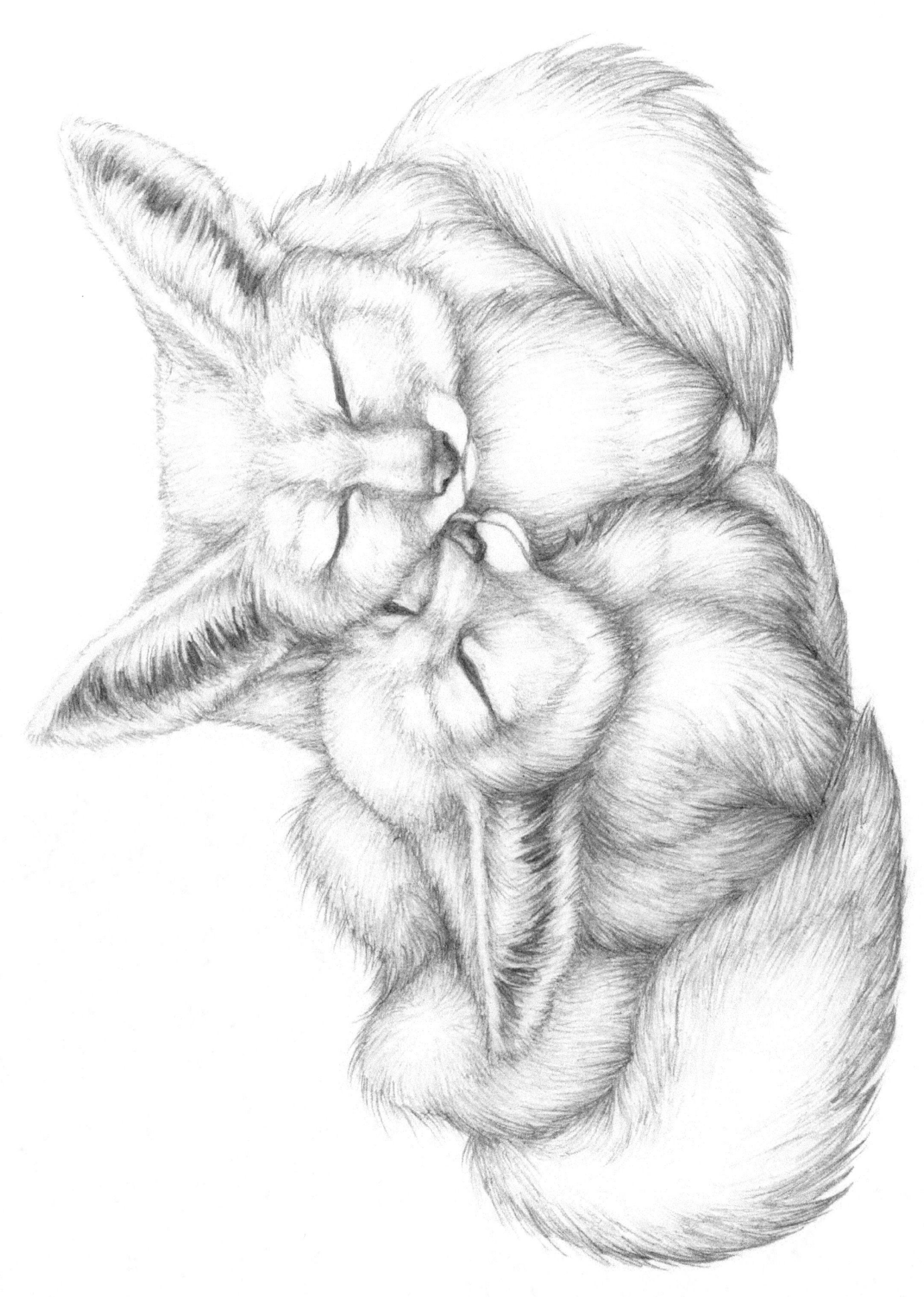

COLOR LOG

THIS IS YOUR SPACE TO TEST COLOR SCHEMES AND LOG
WHAT COLORS YOU USED FOR THE PAGES INSIDE THE
BOOK. HAVE FUN AND EXPERIMENT !!

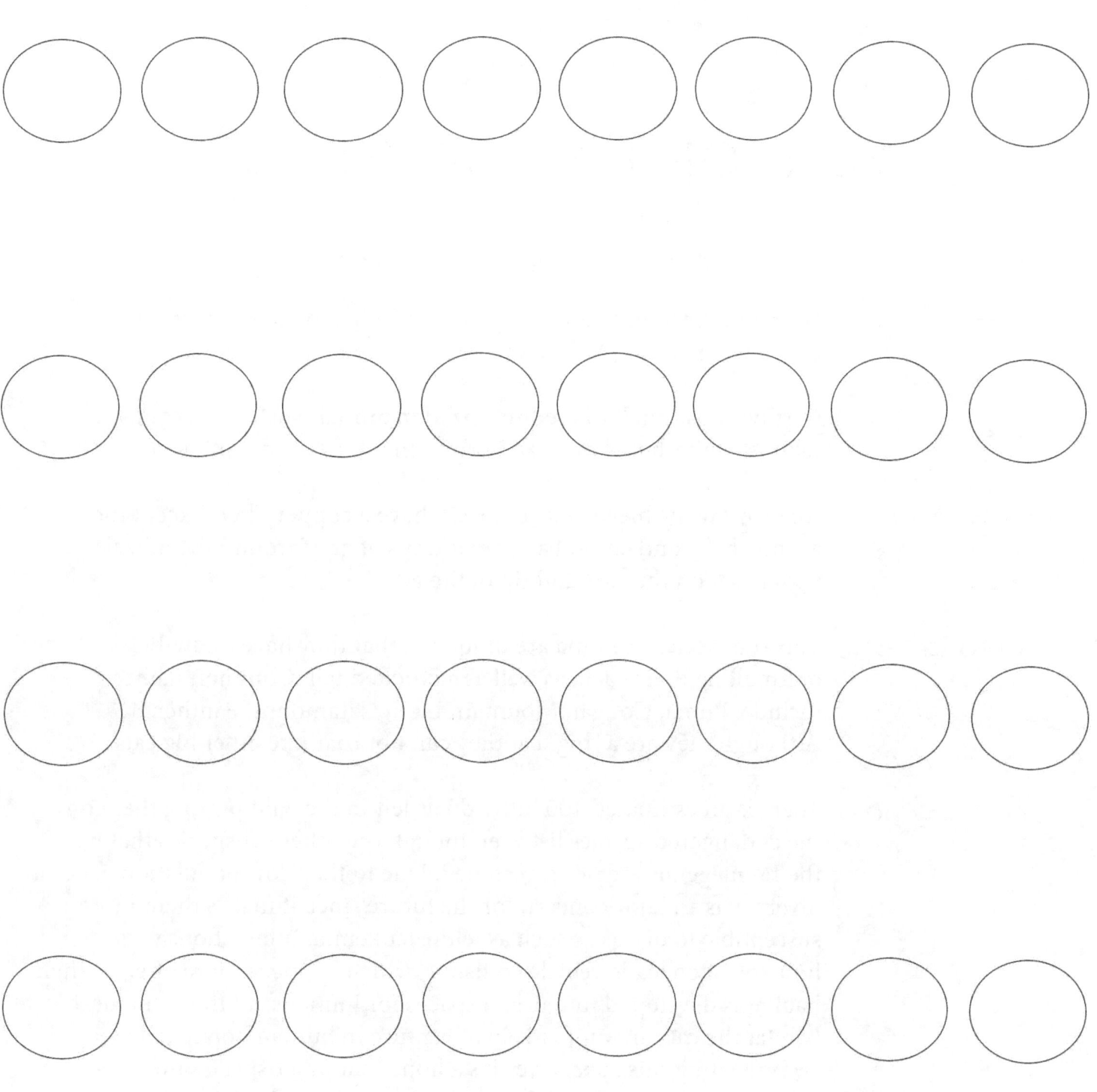

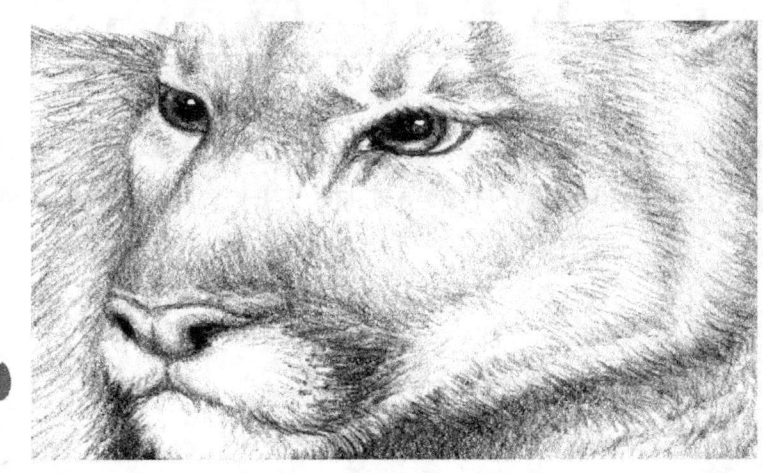

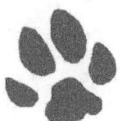 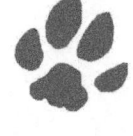

FLORIDA PANTHER
SCIENTIFIC NAME:
PUMA CONCOLOR CORYI

HABITAT: Found in the Southwestern tip of Florida in North America. They prefer warm swamplands, wetlands and upland forests.

DIET: Carnivorous; small to medium sized mammals such as raccoons, rabbits, white-tailed deer, and sometimes birds and reptiles.

COLORATION: All over tawny biege, but some will have a coppery hue, except for a white belly and chest. Facial markings of gray around the muzzle, with black on the ears and tip of the tail.

UNIQUENESS: This subspecies of Puma are unique in that they have a cow-lick of fur along their back, as well as a crooked tail. Common names include: Puma, Cougar, Mountain Lion, Catamount, Panther. Although they are a "big" cat they can not roar like other big cats.

CONSERVATION: There is an estimated 100 individuals left in the wild putting them on the endangered species list even though the other subspecies that up the Puma genus are not threatened. Due to their low population genetic diversity is a major concern for the future since it makes them more susceptible to disease.s such as feline leukemia. Interactions with humans often leads vehicle collisons, which happens more often as their habitat is developed into urban spaces for humans. With less natural habitat the cats are more likely to venture in human populated areas. By protecting this subspecies it's a hope that other species in their habitat are also protected, because they are an umbrella species.

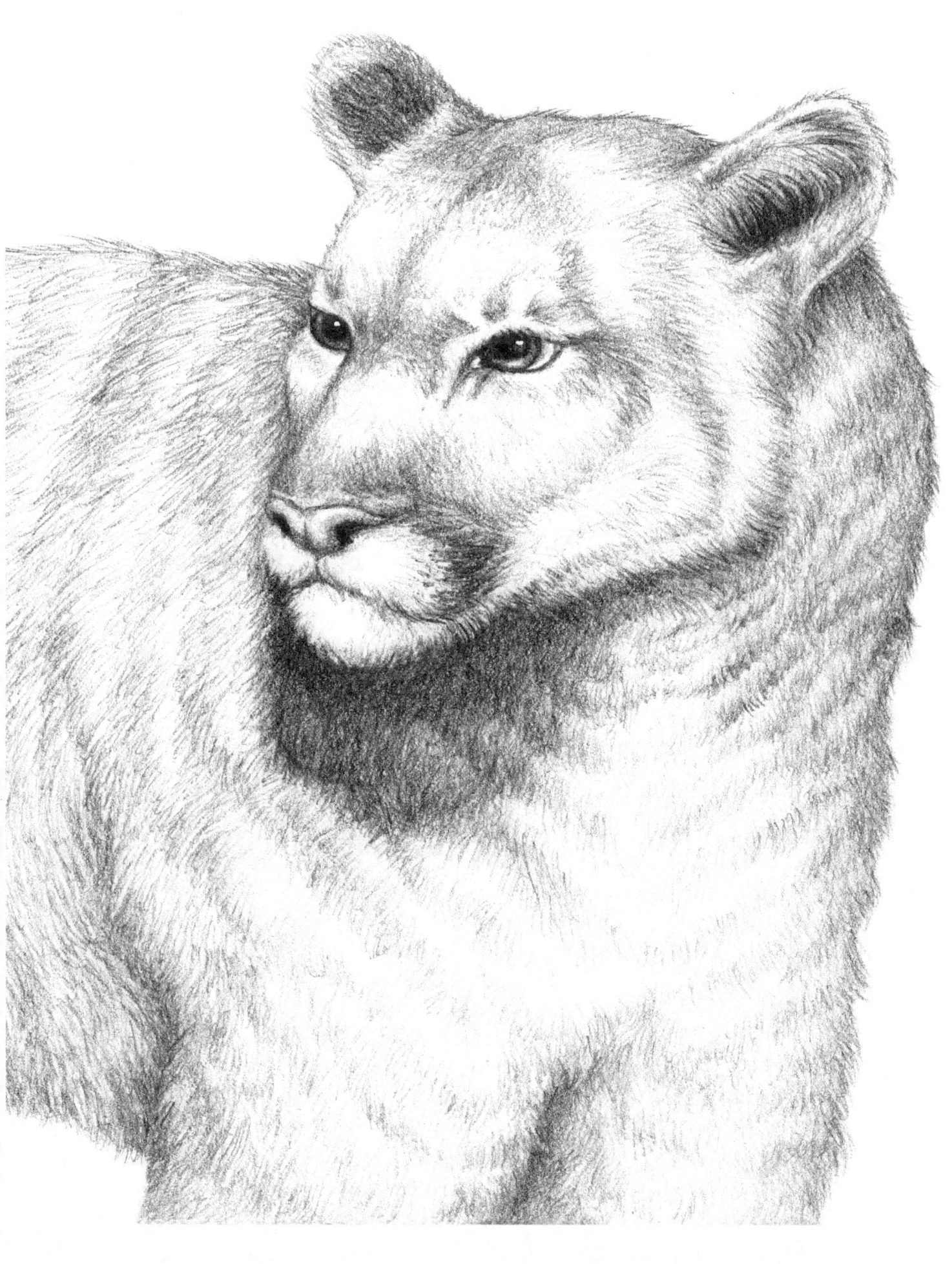

COLOR LOG

THIS IS YOUR SPACE TO TEST COLOR SCHEMES AND LOG
WHAT COLORS YOU USED FOR THE PAGES INSIDE THE
BOOK. HAVE FUN AND EXPERIMENT !!

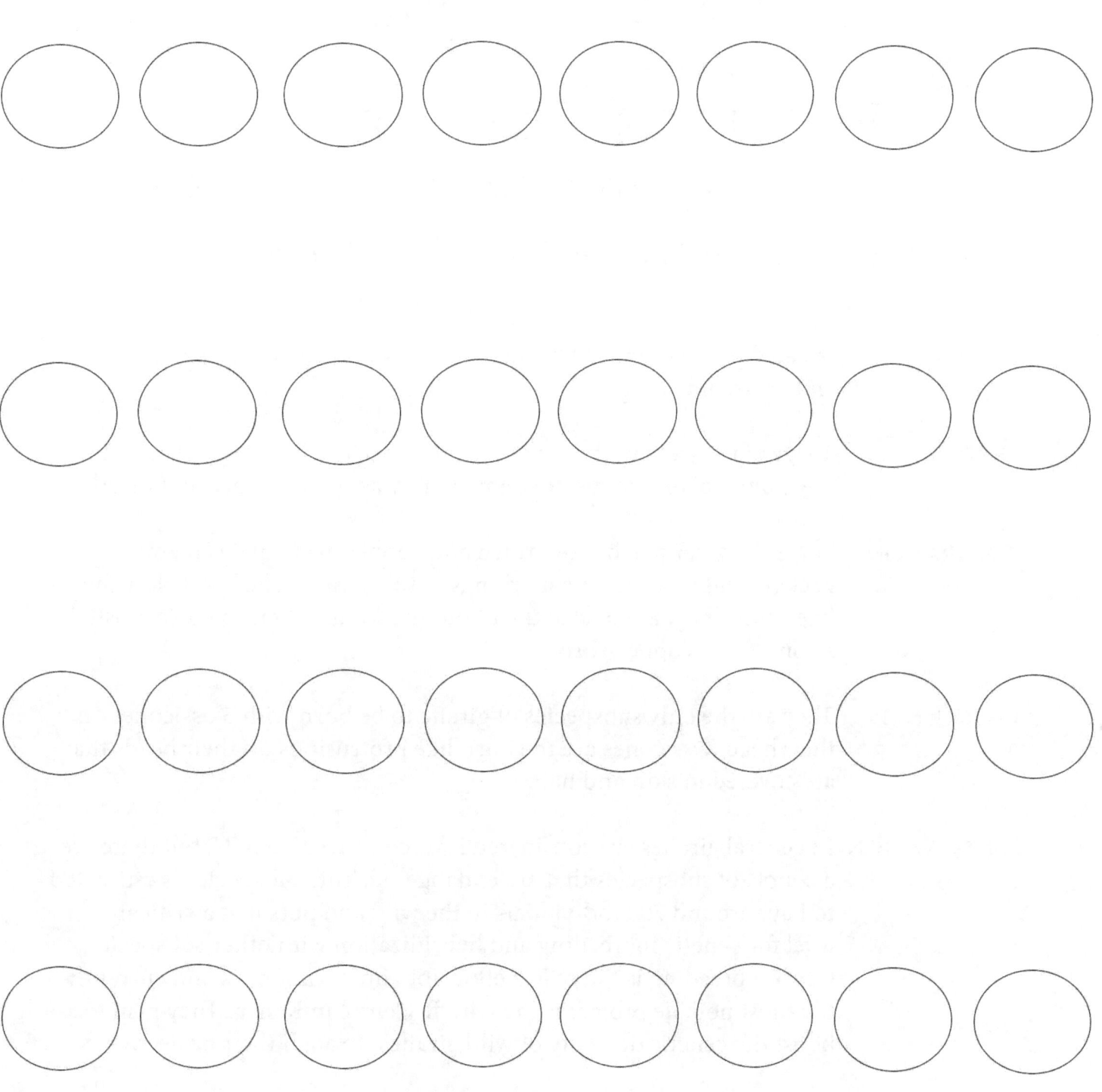

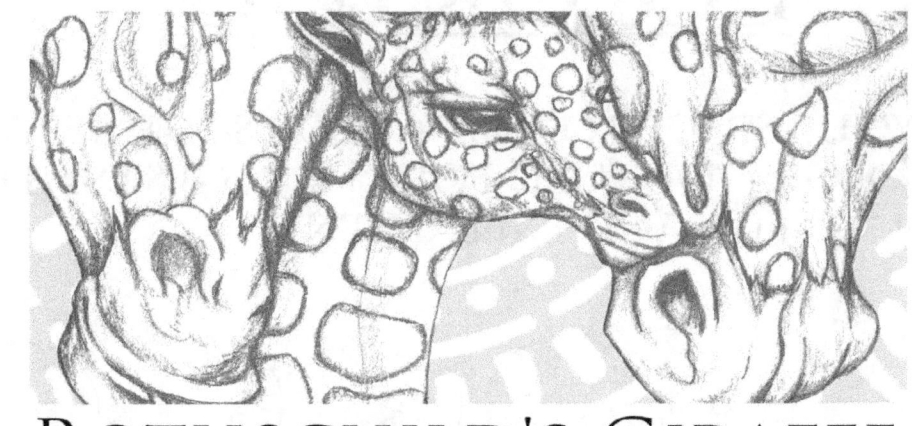

Rothschild's Giraffe

Scientific Name:

Giraffa camelopardalis rothschildi

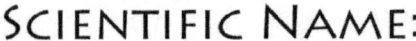

HABITAT: Isolated populations in Uganda and Kenya among the savannahs and grasslands.

DIET: Twigs of the trees in the *Acacia* genus as well as flowering plants in the *Commiphora* genus, the same family as frankincence and myrrh.

COLORATION: Large irregular patches of brown and copper over a pale cream background make up the markings of this giraffe. The legs below the knee and elbow are pale and without markings. Their mane is mostly a completely coppery brown.

UNIQUENESS: They are the only subspecies of giraffe to be born with 5 ossicones on their head. Ossicones are the horn like protrusions on their heads that are covered in skin and hair.

CONSERVATION: In general giraffes are considered least concern by ICUN, but there are a couple of subspecies that are endangered. This subspecies is estimated to have around 700 individuals in the wild and puts it at a critical level for genetic inbreeding and hybridization with other subspecies. Captive breeding is the major effort for conservationists and currently the most notable project is the Giraffe Centre in Kenya. They plan to boost the genetic diversity of wild giraffes through their project.

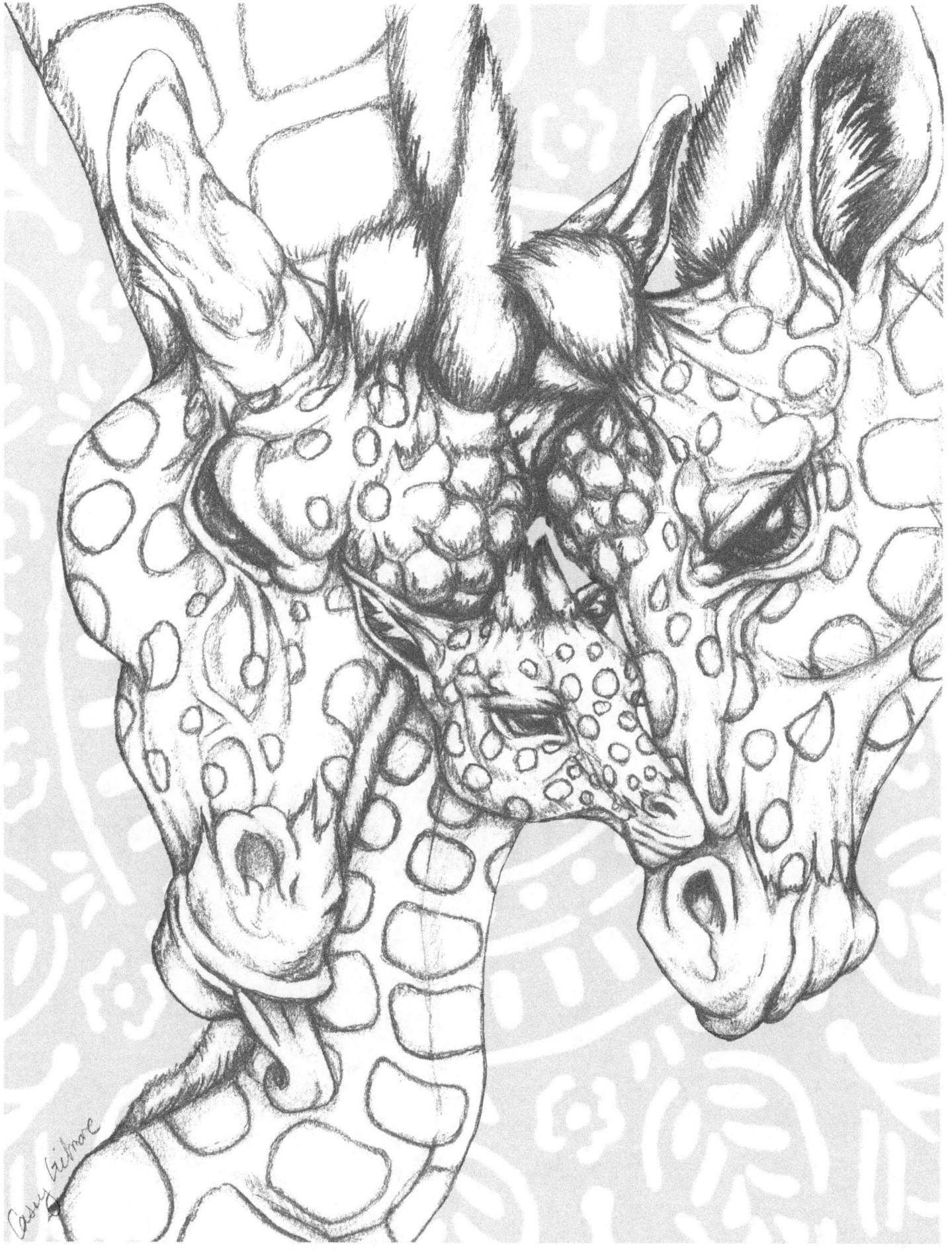

COLOR LOG

THIS IS YOUR SPACE TO TEST COLOR SCHEMES AND LOG
WHAT COLORS YOU USED FOR THE PAGES INSIDE THE
BOOK. HAVE FUN AND EXPERIMENT !!

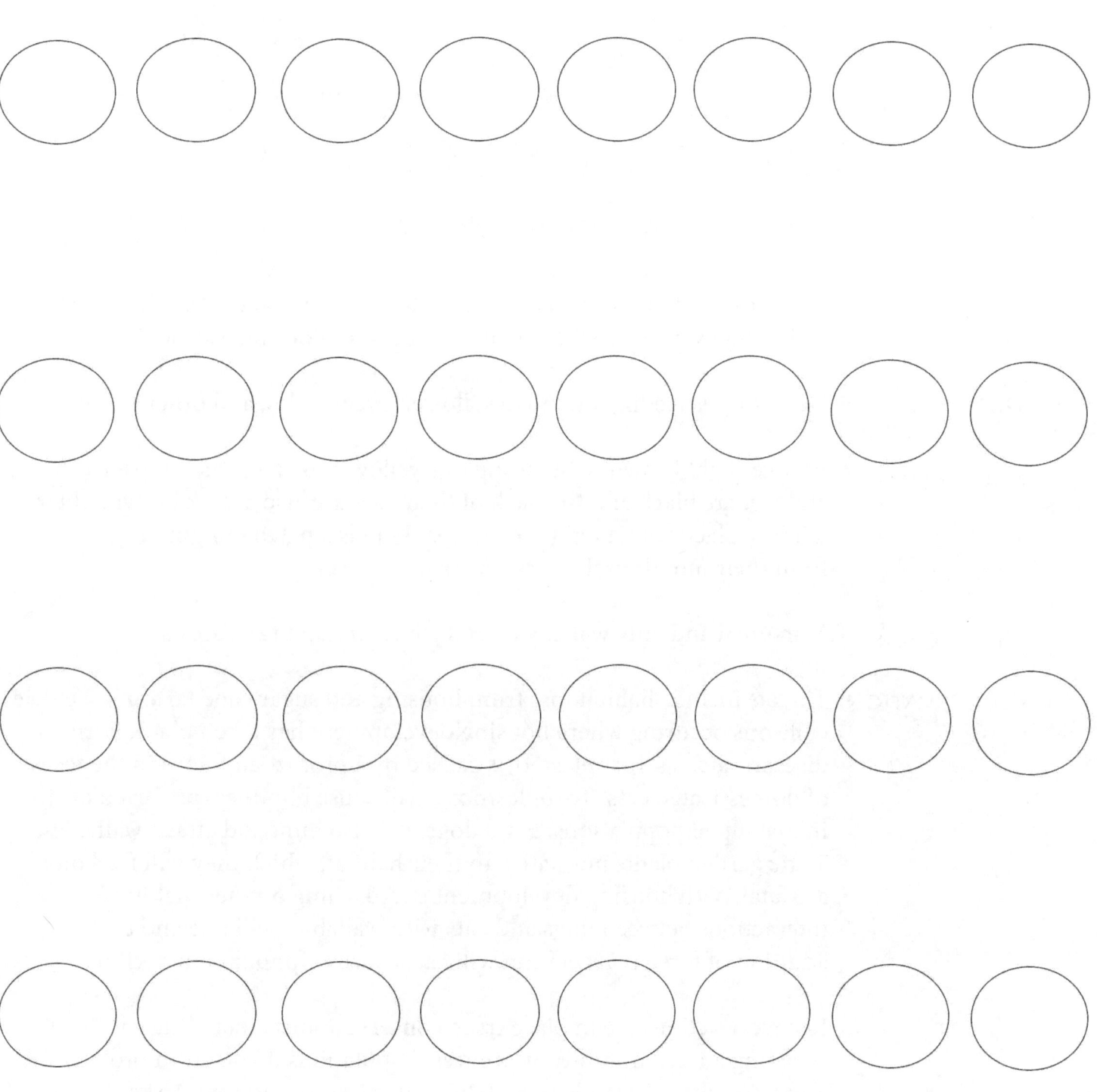

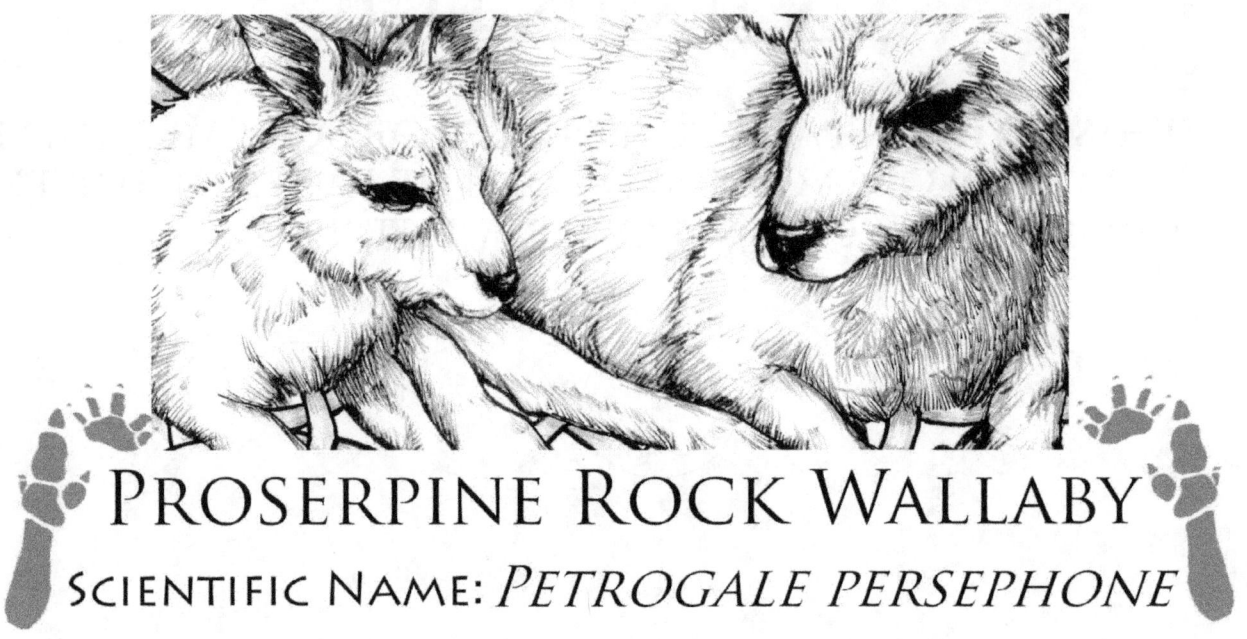

Proserpine Rock Wallaby
Scientific Name: *Petrogale persephone*

Habitat: Dry rainforest of Queensland, Australia; among boulder crevices, rock cliffs, and overhangs with adequate places to hide and escape the heat.

Diet: Herbivorous feeding on grasses, flowers, vegetables, and other foliage.

Coloration: All over light brown with fading to a yellow-brown on the limbs. Paws and feet are black and the back of their ears are also a dark brown. Their tails are black with a light cream tip. There is a patch of light gray from their mouth to the ears across their cheeks.

Uniqueness: Marsupial and only wallaby to exclusively inhabit rainforests.

Conservation: Threats include habitat loss from housing and sugar cane farming. Vehicle collisons occuring where housing development has taken place. Foriegn diseases such as Toxoplasmosis caused by a protozoan found in the feces of domesticated cats. Toxoplasmosis will cause blindness and even death in marsupial populations. Feral dogs will also hunt and attack wallabies. Toxic garden plants not native to their habitat, which they will feed on are fatal. With housing development encroaching on their habitat interactions between dogs and cats with wallabies will rise and the addition of foreign vegetation will cause farther population decline.

Recovery actions are in place from conservationists including captive breeding and community awareness. Populations do occur in protected areas; Conway, Dryander, and Gloucester Island National Parks.

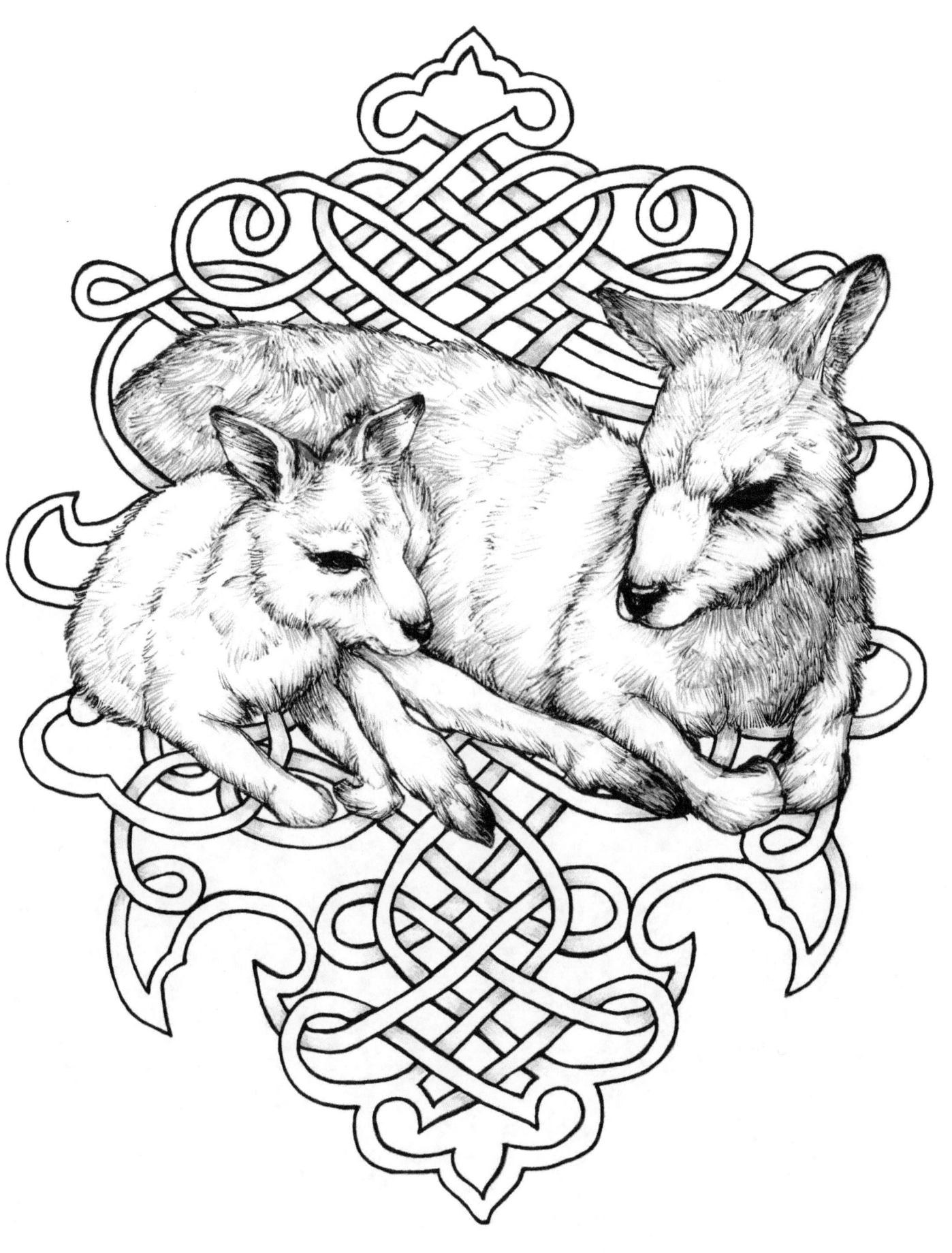

COLOR LOG

THIS IS YOUR SPACE TO TEST COLOR SCHEMES AND LOG
WHAT COLORS YOU USED FOR THE PAGES INSIDE THE
BOOK. HAVE FUN AND EXPERIMENT !!

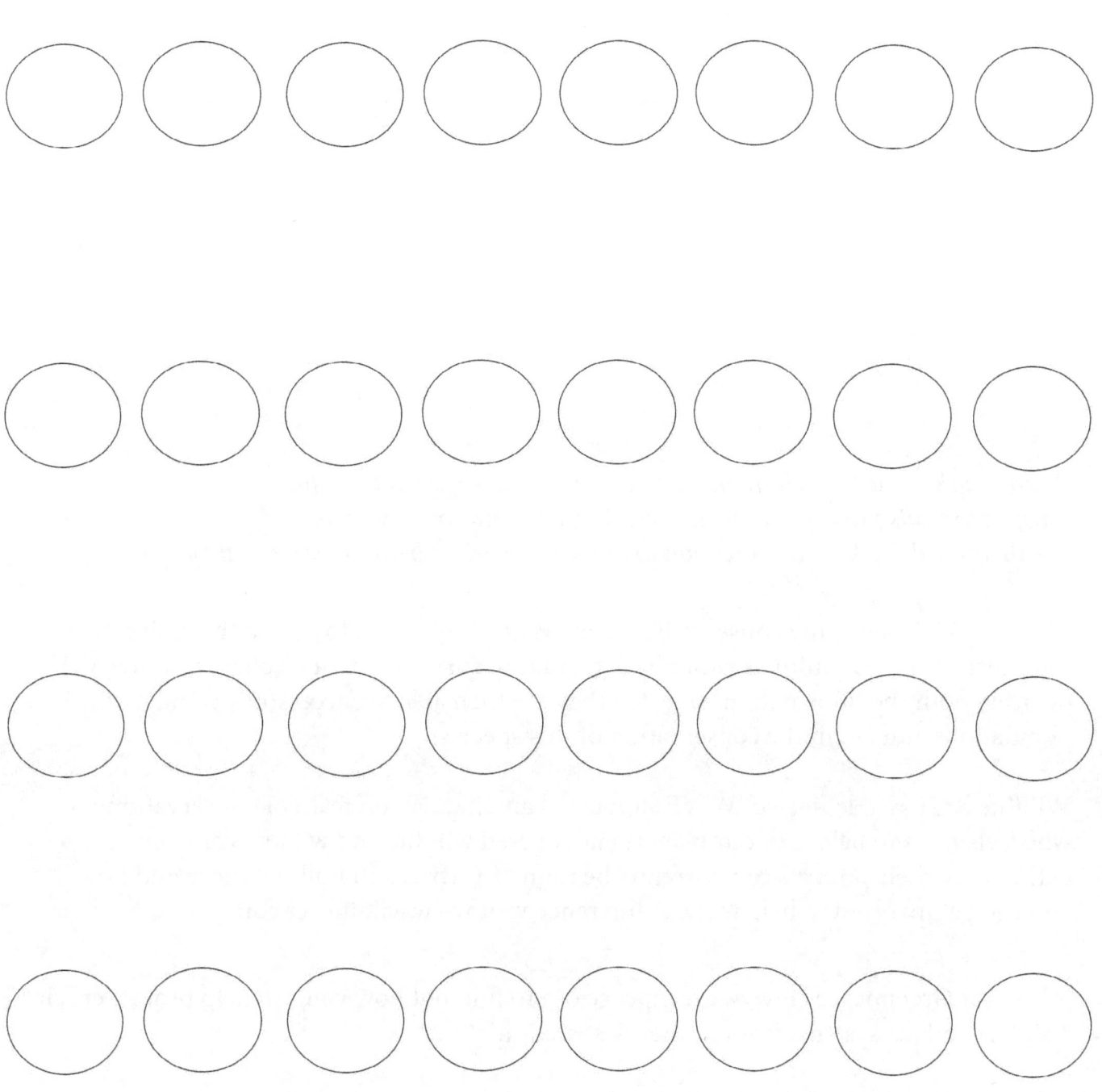

A SPECIAL THANKS TO ALL PATRONS WHO HELPED TO FUND THIS PROJECT

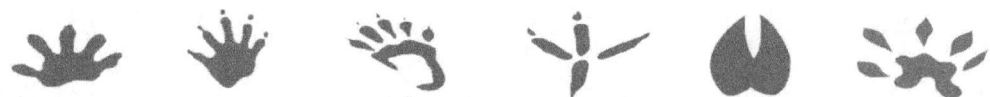

Farther acknowledgement to the following featured organizations for their aid in this project with their special insight into conservation, and for their hard work, and dedication to make the world a better place for all of us.

Wildlife ACT is helping conserve (Cheetah/Wild Dog) in South Africa through active monitoring of these animals either by camera trap surveys, satellite collars or other VHF devices. With the information collected they are then able to successfully monitor the populations and aid in the conservation of this species.

Wildlife ACT is a dedicated, WWF supported and hands - on team of conservationists who's vision is to help save our planets endangered wildlife and wild places from extinction. Their projects can currently be found in Africa. To find out more and how you can get involved to help make a difference visit www.wildlifeact.com

Also visit Greenpeace at www.greenpeace.org to find out how you can help protect crucial habitats and ecosystems from farther destruction.

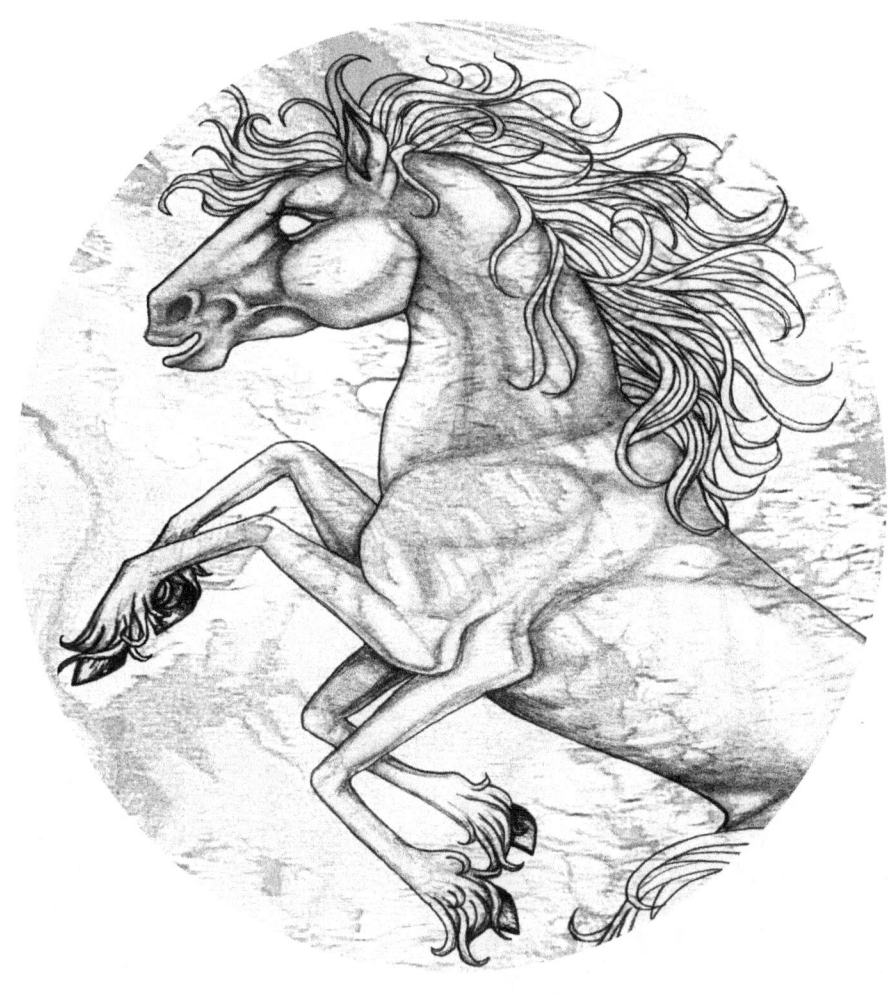

For more information on all things Keyesay
please follow me at my facebook artist page:

https://www.facebook.com/keyesaysfineart

Online store: https://www.etsy.com/shop/KeyesaysVisualArt

Also all other social media sites look for "Keyesay"

www.ingramcontent.com/pod-product-compliance
Lightning Source LLC
Chambersburg PA
CBHW080719190526
45169CB00006B/2435